# The Picture Book of Kids' Crafts and Activities

# The Picture Book of Kids' Crafts and Activities

Roxanne Henderson

Illustrated by Michael Brown
and Cassio Lynm

Produced by The Philip Lief Group, Inc.

**CB**
CONTEMPORARY BOOKS

**Library of Congress Cataloging-in-Publication Data**

Henderson, Roxanne
    The picture book of kids' crafts and activities : more than 200
terrific projects fully illustrated for easy reference / Roxanne
Henderson : illustrated by Michael Brown and Cassio Lynm : produced
by The Philip Lief Group, Inc.
        p.   cm.
    ISBN 0-8092-2968-4
    1.  Handicraft.   I.  Title.
TT157.H39    1998
745.5—dc21                                      97-50344
                                                           CIP

Cover design by Monica Baziuk
Interior design by Michael Brown and Cassio Lynm

Published by Contemporary Books
A division of NTC/Contemporary Publishing Group, Inc.
4255 West Touhy Avenue, Lincolnwood (Chicago), Illinois 60646-1975 U.S.A.
Printed in the United States of America
International Standard Book Number: 0-8092-2968-4

18   17   16   15   14   13   12   11   10   9   8   7   6   5   4   3   2   1

This book is dedicated to my mother, Jean,
who has used her talent for crafts to make
so many beautiful gifts for the people she loves.

# Acknowledgments

The libraries near my home hold many hundreds of books, many dating back to other centuries, that are filled with recipes, ideas, and instructions for craft making from teachers, artists, writers, and parents. To some extent, this book collects the best of these and would not be nearly as rich without the many others who took the time to write down their ideas. It also would not have been possible without the ideas and influence of my husband, Michael, an artist and art teacher who understands how the minds of children approach the materials of craft making. Finally, I owe a great thanks to the quick intelligence and nimble drawing hand of Cassio Lynm, who transformed my ideas so effortlessly into clear and graceful images.

# Contents

## IV.  In the Kitchen  193

## V.  Fabric, Yarn, Ribbon, and String  227

# The Picture Book of Kids' Crafts and Activities

# Introduction

Ask kids what they like best about school, and one of the most frequent answers will be "art class." Not only does art class have no multiplication tables or spelling tests, but also it's a place where kids learn how to make some pretty cool things, and that's a lot of fun. Kids love the freedom and self-direction of arts and crafts, and they love handling all the different materials. A child who's mashing, squeezing, cutting, tearing, sanding, bending, smearing, twisting, or braiding is a happy child. Most of all, kids like being creative and making something that is uniquely their own, and they are always proud of the objects and pictures they create with their own hands.

The lucky ones keep this love of crafts as a source of pleasure and relaxation for the rest of their lives. Indeed, many of the activities in this book, such as weaving, origami, and plaster of paris modeling, are based on art forms and hobbies that have been enjoyed by adults for centuries. We present them in a form that's simple enough for youngsters of 10 or 12 to do on their own, and younger children can enjoy them just as much with a little more help from adults. For kids as young as 5 or 6 and the adults in their lives, *The Picture Book of Kids' Crafts and Activities* will serve both as a primer for many traditional crafts and as an introduction to dozens of craft and tabletop activities that many readers have never encountered before.

## What's in This Book

This book contains 140 entries that describe how to make more than 200 arts-and-crafts objects, toys, optical illusions, and even things to wear and eat! Each entry includes step-by-step instructions, and each step is illustrated. Some of these projects are quite simple, requiring just a few materials and a few moments to complete.

Others are more challenging, either intellectually (it takes a bit of concentration to create an origami duck), physically (can you believe some grownups never mastered simple braiding?), or in the amount of time required (when drying flowers, you must be patient).

One thing is certain: there is something for everyone. In this book we start out with some tips for quickly improving drawing and painting skills, and then we describe a huge variety of printing, stenciling, bookmaking, and other paper projects. We include instructions for a large group of three-dimensional objects using paper, doughs, clays and plasters, and many other media. In this book you'll also find a number of ways to work with nature's bounty, from preserving flowers to making jewelry from seeds. You can help a child build a sturdy wooden birdhouse and an almost-instant bird feeder. We provide simple stitching and braiding and weaving instructions and offer a great assortment of fun food treats to build for birthday parties—and much more!

## How to Use This Book

Have you ever looked at a list of supplies you need to help your child complete a craft project and decided to rent a video instead? Have you ever read through the instructions for a craft and thought, "Huh?"? That won't happen when you use *The Picture Book of Kids' Crafts and Activities*. We make it easy for you to figure out exactly what materials you'll need, and often these are things you already have around the house. We tell you where to start and offer a picture for each step, so you always know precisely what to do next until you have a finished product.

Look over the table of contents and notice that the projects are grouped in chapters and sections according to the kind of activity (print-making, sculpting, and so on) and the materials you'll use (foodstuffs, fabric). In addition, each entry begins with a list that outlines the basics of the project. The list includes:

**Type of Activity** (sculpting, sewing, and so on)
**Object** (what your goal or completed project will be or do)
**Ages** (who can get the most from this activity)
**Materials Needed** (including tools such as scissors; supplies of paper and glue; and sometimes protective materials such as coverings for work surfaces and mitts for cooking. Most of our materials can be bought at your corner discount store; a few are found only in specialty stores. Unless a particular type of paint or glue is called for, you can use whatever you have or improvise.)

**A note on age recommendations:** We suggest a minimum age for crafters of each project, but in reality, different kids will need different amounts of hands-on help. Children even younger than the suggested age may enjoy being involved in the activity, but they will need significantly more help from adults at each step. Also, in some cases what seems to be an inappropriately low age appears for a project. For instance, an activity such as Soap Crayons obviously cannot be completed by 5-year-olds working alone. However, we suggest the project for that age group because playing with the crayons is the perfect playtime activity for those kids. Also,

look for the notation "Adult Supervision" in certain entries. This means that for kids not yet in their teens, adults should be on the scene during the use of a cookstove, an iron, knives, bleach, or other dangerous items. We give no cut-off age, since many of these projects are just as much fun for teenagers and adults as they are for kids. Finally, remember that craft makers of all ages bring varying levels of skill and interest to particular activities. Ultimately, parents and teachers will be the best judges of what an individual kid can do and will enjoy.

## Have Fun!

This book offers many creative alternatives to electronic entertainment. It will serve parents, camp counselors, teachers, and any others who want to have some worthwhile good times with their kids. It is the book to reach for when you are wondering what to do on a rainy day—or any day. But, always remember, the real goal of every activity in this book is to have fun!

We provide you with a wealth of activities to choose from, all with simple instructions. We hope that this book, like your favorite and most well-worn cookbook, will lead the way not just to success with individual craft projects, but also to developing the confidence and knowledge to master many crafts skills. Use our "recipes" as a starting point, but don't be afraid to experiment. This is just the beginning!

# I. Art Aplenty

## Drawing and Painting Basics

Most everyone enjoys drawing and painting, and that's great because these activities are really the fundamentals of all artwork. The more skill you develop in drawing and painting, the more fun you'll have doing many of the craft projects in this book. Good skills also make it easier to give all your craft work a personal and unique touch. The following activities are designed to help you learn some useful techniques.

# Drawing Basics

**Materials Needed:**
- At least six sheets of unlined paper, 8½ by 11 inches or larger
- Objects to draw (a shoe, potted plant, or stuffed animal, for instance)
- Pencils: regular (#2), soft, and extra soft
- At least two sheets of paper about 11 by 17 inches
- An eraser
- A table lamp *or* large flashlight

**Type of Activity:** Drawing
**Object:** Learn five simple ways to improve your drawing skill
**Ages:** 9 and older

## #1 The Building Block Way to Draw

**1** Seat yourself comfortably at a table. Arrange a sheet of paper in front of you with your chosen object a few feet away.

**2** Use your #2 pencil to draw the object's most basic geometric shapes—squares and circles. Use light lines, and just try to capture the basic overall shape of the object.

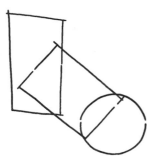

**3** Fill out these shapes, and begin to add details. Use darker lines, but still be sketchy.

**4** Finally, darken and refine the details, then erase the "building block" shapes.

## #2 The Concentrated Way to Draw

**1** Seat yourself comfortably at a table. Arrange your paper in front of you, with your object a few feet away. With a #2 pencil, starting from the middle of the top of the object, use a single, careful line to draw the entire outline. Look from one detail to the next, and imagine your drawing hand crawling along the edges of the object.

**2** Concentrate; move your pencil slowly. Use a single line to show the edge of each part of the shoe. Don't erase—don't worry about "accuracy." This exercise helps you learn to concentrate and develop an artist's eye.

**Hint:** Too much erasing will ruin your effort. Slow down. Look carefully. You should be spending more time looking at the object you are drawing than actually moving the pencil. You are learning to concentrate and to draw what you see. Don't worry if efforts don't come out exactly "right."

# #3  Drawing Shadows and Using Shading

**1** Lay a large sheet of paper down on the table. Crease a second sheet in the middle and stand it on its end on top of the first sheet.

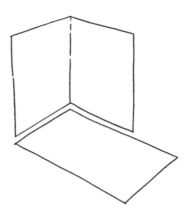

**2** Set your object in front of the standing paper. Turn off overhead lights. Turn on your lamp, and arrange it so that it casts a shadow of the object against the standing paper.

**3** On a separate sheet of paper, draw the shadows cast on the paper. You may want to draw the outline with your #2 pencil, and shade with a softer-lead pencil.

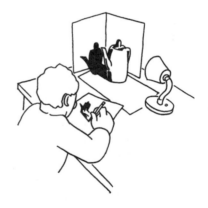

**4** Also draw the shapes of the shadows that occur on your object. Notice that the shadows are not fuzzy and they appear on various parts of the object, not just along the edges. Shadows have definite shape and can be cast anywhere on an object.

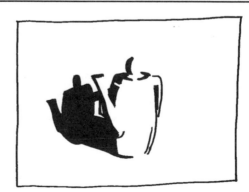

## #4  Simple Perspective

**1** On an 8½-by-11-inch sheet of paper, draw a tree. (Copy the one shown here or create your own.) Make it fairly large, near the bottom of the page.

**2** To the right, draw the same tree, this one higher up on the page and about half the size of the first drawing.

**3** Draw it again, higher and smaller still. Draw a horizon line.

**4** On a fresh sheet of paper, make the drawing again, this time overlapping the objects so that the smaller ones are partially hidden. Add any other objects or details (such as grass) you'd like to complete the picture.

**5** You can add larger objects in the foreground. See how realistically things seem to disappear into the "distance"?

# #5 Drawing Things in Motion

**Other Materials Needed:**
• A friend to be your model

**1** Ask a friend to perform movements for you—running, bending, and so on. Ask him or her to freeze in mid-movement.

**2** Give yourself 5 minutes only to draw the pose on a fresh sheet of paper. Draw quickly at first, and don't worry about details such as hair or clothing.

A sketchy, lively drawing beats a detailed, stiff one any day.

# Painting Basics

**Materials Needed:**

- Sturdy white paper
- A pencil
- Water-soluble paint in tubes or jars: poster, tempera, acrylic, *or* watercolors; you can buy all the colors you want, but the only colors you must have are black, white, red, yellow, and blue
- A small plastic tub *or* other container for holding water and washing brushes
- A palette, such as a cafeteria tray, an old cookie sheet, *or* a paper *or* plastic plate
- Assorted sizes and types of brushes
- A plastic water bottle
- Rags *or* paper towels
- A carryall *or* backpack
- Objects to paint (such as fruits and vegetables)
- Photos of your choice

**Type of Activity:** Painting
**Object:** Learn four simple ways to get started painting
**Ages:** 8 and older

## #1 Getting Started with Paint

**1** Pack your painting materials and fill your water bottle.

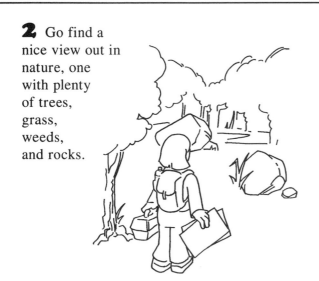

**2** Go find a nice view out in nature, one with plenty of trees, grass, weeds, and rocks.

**3** Put a small amount of black paint on your palette and pour some water into the tub.

**4** Experiment with mixing different amounts of water into the paint, dipping your brush into the tub to add water. On your paper, test various mixtures of paint and water. Notice the various kinds of marks and the different levels of control you have with different thicknesses of paint.

**5** Try each brush. Use what you have observed about the different thicknesses of paint and brushes to capture the shades and textures of the landscape around you. For now, just play at making a landscape with black paint as you learn to control the paint and brushes.

# #2 Color Wheel

**1** Draw a circle, then another one inside it. Divide them into six pie pieces.

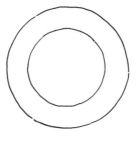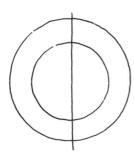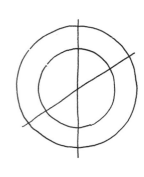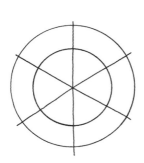

**2** Put about a spoonful each of red, blue, yellow, and white on your palette. Then paint your color wheel as follows, using the palette, not the wheel, for mixing the paint, and making sure to rinse your brush with water and clean it with a rag or paper towel when changing colors:

- Red paint in the inner half of one of the pie pieces; red mixed with white (pink) in the outer rim.
- Skip a pie piece. Put blue on the inside wedge and a mix of blue and white (sky blue) on the outer rim.
- Skip a pie piece. Put yellow on the inside wedge and yellow and white (pale yellow) on the outer rim.

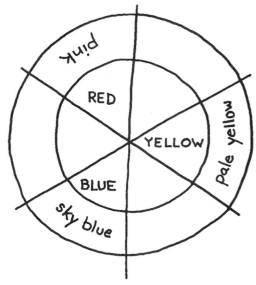

**3** Now paint in the remaining pie pieces:

- Between the red and blue segments, mix red and blue to make purple. Add white to purple for lavender in the outer rim of this segment.
- Between the red and yellow segments, mix red and yellow to make orange. Add white to the orange for the outer rim (peach).
- Between the yellow and blue segments, mix yellow and blue to get green. Add white to green for the outer rim (lime green).

Notice which colors are opposite each other on the wheel. For instance, orange is opposite blue. When mixing paint, if you want to darken blue, add orange (not black). This is true for all opposites. Give it a try.

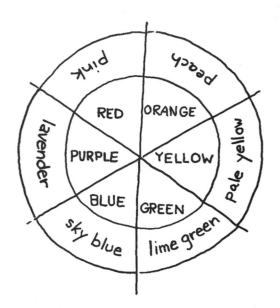

**4** You can also divide the circle into 12 parts instead of 6 by dividing each of your pie pieces in half again. Mix more subtle variations, imitating the basic steps just shown. Remember that you can add white to any new color, as you did before.

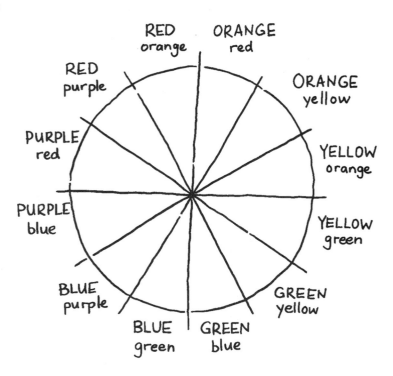

# #3 Mixing Colors While Painting a Picture

**1** Assemble a colorful still life. Fruits and vegetables are a good subject. Sketch the basic shapes. Don't go into detail.

**2** Use the lessons learned in the preceding Color Wheel to mix paints on your palette to match the colors of the fruits and vegetables. Paint the fruits you've drawn.

**Hint:** Don't forget to add the right amount of water to the paint for the effect and control you're after.

# #4  Making the Mood Right

**1** Choose a photo or picture from a magazine for your subject.

**2** Sketch the subject.

**3** Paint it, using only red, orange, yellow (the warm colors), and white.

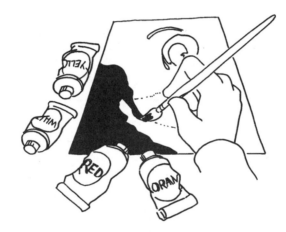

**4** Sketch it again, and paint it using the cool colors of blue and green, with white.

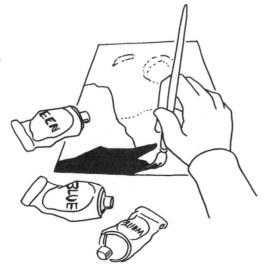

## Variations:

Try other limited color schemes, such as all dark colors (good for mountain scenes), or all colors mixed heavily with white (a sunny beach mood).

# Fun Fingerpaints

**Type of Activity:** Making paint
**Object:** Make your own paints for fingerpainting fun
**Ages:** 6 and older—*Adult Supervision*

**Materials Needed:**
- A medium-size saucepan
- ½ cup of all-purpose (not self-rising) white flour
- 2 cups of water
- A big stirring spoon
- 1 tablespoon of glycerin
- Three small containers with lids
- Red, yellow, and blue food coloring
- Extra-large sheets of smooth, thick paper
- A palette, such as a cafeteria tray, an old cookie sheet, *or* a paper or plastic plate

**1** Place the flour in the saucepan, and slowly add the water, stirring continually until all the lumps are gone.

**2** Cook the mixture over low heat, stirring constantly, until it is clear and thick.

**3** Remove the pan from the heat and let the mixture cool, then add the glycerin. Stir in a bit more water if the mixture seems too thick; it should be about like mayonnaise.

**4** Divide the mixture into the three containers, and color each batch with the food colors. (The paints will keep for a week or so, covered and refrigerated.)

**5** Spread out your paper and paints, flex your fingers, and have fun.

**Hint:** Use the Color Wheel exercise (page 11) to guide you in mixing all the extra colors you need on your palette.

# Quick Silhouette

**Materials Needed:**
- Paper measuring 11 by 17 inches or larger
- Removable tape
- The subject—a friendly helper
- A chair, lamp, and table
- A pencil *or* colored marker

**Type of Activity:** Drawing
**Object:** Make a portrait of a friend
**Ages:** 10 and older

**1** Tape your paper to the wall, and seat your friend in front of and perpendicular to it. Place the lamp on the table, remove the shade, then turn the lamp on. Line up the table, lamp, and subject so that a sharp silhouette of your friend appears on the paper.

**2** Trace the outline of the head.

**3** Fill in the head shape.

## Variation:

Use the collage or printing techniques described later in this chapter to make a meaningful background around the head.

# Optical Illusion

**Materials Needed:**
- Two 3-by-5-inch unlined index cards *or* slips of paper
- A pencil *or* pen

**Type of Activity:** Drawing
**Object:** Create the illusion of a bird in a cage
**Ages:** 10 and older

**1** On one of the cards, draw a bird and, beside it, a cage.

**2** Hold the second card straight up with one of its 3-inch edges resting between the cage and the bird.

**3** Touch the bridge of your nose to the upright card so that you're looking down at the bird with one eye and the cage with the other eye. Keep looking; be patient.

**4** The bird hops into the cage!

## Variations:
- Draw a face and a window.
- Draw a fishbowl and a fish.

# Rubbing, Printing, Stenciling, Photocopying, and More

# Good Impressions

**Materials Needed:**
- An object from which to take an impression (see step 1)
- Thin paper (typing, onion skin, tissue, tracing)
- Scissors
- Removable tape
- Crayons, pastels, *or* charcoal

**Type of Activity:** Paper rubbing
**Object:** Create a good, clear impression of an interesting object
**Ages:** 7 and older

**1** Choose a relatively flat, stiff object with an interesting texture. A coin is good, a scallop-type shell, a leaf, a feather—whatever is at hand. Cut a piece of paper slightly larger than the object you'll be rubbing.

**2** Arrange the object on your working surface. You can use rolled-over tape to hold it in place if you like. Spread the paper over the object, and tape the edges of the paper to the work surface.

**3** Rub the crayon over the paper. Keep the pressure gentle and even for a smooth appearance.

**4** You may rub only to the edge of the object. This way, the design stands out on the blank page.

**5** *Or*, rub all the way to the edge of the page for a different look.

## Variation:
Use a large sheet of paper, and cover it with rubbings of many related objects.

# Styrofoam Block Print

**Type of Activity:** Paper printing
**Object:** Make a printing block for creating a repeated design
**Ages:** 8 and older—*Adult Supervision*

**Materials Needed:**
- Paper
- A pencil
- Scissors
- A sheet *or* block of styrofoam, at least 1½ inches thick
- A sharp knife
- A thick paintbrush *or* sponge
- Paint *or* washable ink, not thick and not watery
- A saucer *or* jar lid to use as a dipping pot for the paint
- Newspaper *or* scrap paper
- Peel-and-stick mailing labels (for Variation #2)

**1** Draw a design on paper, and cut it out. (Or you could photocopy a design and cut that out.)

**2** Trace the cutout design onto the styrofoam.

**3** Use the knife to carefully carve the outline of your design, cutting straight down ¼ to ½ inch.

**4** Cut away the styrofoam from outside of the design until only the raised design remains. Smooth away any styrofoam crumbs.

**5** Use the brush or sponge to dab paint onto the surface of your printing block.

**6** Press the block firmly but gently onto your paper.

**7** There's your design! (This is a *positive* print.)

**Hint:** Before printing on good-quality paper, practice a few times on newspaper to get the amount of ink and pressure right.

## Variation #1: Negative Print

**1** After step 3, instead of cutting away the styrofoam from the outside of the design, carefully carve the design down into the block.

**2** Paint the ink onto the raised surface that surrounds the design, then make your impression. (This is a *negative* print.)

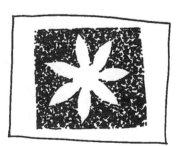

## Variation #2:  Block Printing Personal Stickers on Mailing Labels

**1** Make a block printer small enough for the design to fit on a single label. Your block printer might be a meaningful symbol or your initials.

**2** If you use your initials, make sure to carve them out *backward* so that they will print *forward*.

**3** Print onto the mailing labels. Now you can leave your mark on notebooks, papers, letters—but please, not the furniture!

# Veggie Pix

**Type of Activity:** Paper printing
**Object:** Use a vegetable or fruit to create a
printing block
**Ages:** 9 and older—*Adult Supervision*

**Materials Needed:**
- Fresh produce (bell pepper, cabbage, cauli-
flower, apple slices—be creative!)
- A sharp knife
- A paintbrush *or* sponge
- Non-toxic paint *or* washable ink, not thick and
not watery
- A saucer *or* jar lid to use as a dipping pot for
the paint
- Smooth, sturdy paper
- Scrap paper

**1** Look carefully
at your chosen
fruit or vegetable.
Cut it in a way
that reveals an
interesting surface.
The inner surface of
a cabbage, a halved
bell pepper, and
celery sticks, for
example, serve well
as printing "blocks."

**2** Plan out your
design. Then, with the
brush or sponge, cover
the cut surface of the
veggie thoroughly—
but not drippingly—
with paint or ink.

**3** Press the block
firmly but gently
onto the paper.
There's your design!

**Hint:** Try out
each veg on
scrap paper
before you press
it down onto
your work in
progress.

# Pet-and-Me Prints

**Materials Needed:**
- A gentle-natured dog, cat, parrot, *or* other pet
- A paper plate
- Non-toxic paint *or* washable ink, not thick and not watery
- Large poster paper *or* watercolor paper
- Wet rags

**Type of Activity:** Paper printing
**Object:** Create a personal memento of the family pet
**Ages:** 9 and older

**1** First, give Bowser a big hug.

**2** Spread a layer of paint on the paper plate.

**3** Press your pet pal's paw down onto the paint, then gently onto your printing paper. (Be sure to use the rags to wash the paw before Bowser trots off!)

**4** Press your own hands onto the paint and then onto the paper. You have both your prints, together forever!

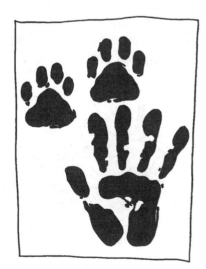

# Impression Printing

**Type of Activity:** Paper printing
**Object:** Make expressionistic "paintings" and interesting designs with common objects
**Ages:** 8 and older

**Materials Needed:**
• An object to use for a printing block (see step 1)
• A paintbrush *or* sponge
• Paint *or* washable ink—must be thick, not watery, and nontoxic
• A saucer *or* jar lid to use as a dipping pot for the paint
• Heavy, smooth poster paper *or* watercolor paper
• Newspaper

**1** You can use a feather, leaf, piece of stiff lace, screen, pot scrubber, or almost anything else. The toy chest, kitchen and bathroom cabinets, junk drawers, and garage hold a wealth of natural printing blocks. Paint one side of the object—say, a leaf—until it's good and wet, but not dripping.

**2** Lay the object painted-side down on blank paper. Put several layers of newspaper on top and press down. Be firm but gentle. Make sure to press all parts down.

**3** Pull up the newspaper and object, and voilà.

## Variation:
Combine several different objects on a large sheet of paper for an interesting effect.

# Spray and Splatter Printing

**Materials Needed:**
- A large cardboard box
- Plain paper cut to fit into the bottom of your box
- Design objects of your choice (see step 1)
- A stiff toothbrush
- Nontoxic paint *or* washable ink
- A bowl *or* jar for the paint or ink
- An empty spray bottle *or* a can of spray paint

**Type of Activity:** Paper printing
**Object:** Make an instant work of art from a common object
**Ages:** 8 and older

**1** Choose some more-or-less flat, interestingly shaped natural objects (leaves, feathers) or household objects (cookie cutters, clothespins). Or, from construction paper draw and cut out a shamrock, heart, key, leaf—anything you like!

**2** Place the plain paper in the bottom of the box, and arrange your objects on it. Do this in a place where paint splatters won't matter.

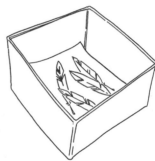

**3** Dip the toothbrush into the container of paint and shake off the excess. With your thumb, flick the paint out of the brush onto the bottom of the box.

**4** Keep refilling the brush and flicking until everything on the bottom of the box is covered with spots and splatters. Pull up your design objects, and you're left with the negative print.

## Variation:
For a different look, instead of toothbrush-splattering, spray your paint. Buy spray paint in the can or put your paint in an old pump-spray bottle. Experiment with several nozzles and various thicknesses of paint for different effects.

# String Along

**Type of Activity:** Paper printing

**Object:** Make instant (and symmetrical) art-work from strands of string

**Ages:** 7 and older

**Materials Needed:**
- Several sheets of sturdy, unlined paper, at least 8½ by 11 inches
- Pieces of string, 15 inches or longer—cotton string, twine, even thin nylon cord will work
- Nontoxic paint *or* washable ink
- A bowl *or* plate for the paint or ink

**1** Fold a sheet of paper in half, either way, then spread it open.

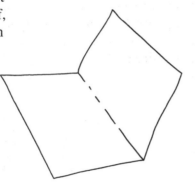

**2** Hold a length of string by one end and dip it into the paint, covering it totally with paint.

**3** Move the string to your paper. Lay it down on half the sheet in loops, curls, or zigs.

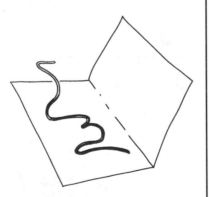

**4** Close the other half of the sheet onto the string. Lightly press it down, then open it and gently lift out the string.

**5** You've got a double abstract image.

## Variations:

Use several strings with different colors, one after another, on one sheet; experiment with fast and slow pulls; use dental floss, yarn, plastic beads, and so on.

# Double-Trouble Rorschach

**Type of Activity:** Paper printing
**Object:** Make instant (and symmetrical) art-
work with paint splatters
**Ages:** 9 and older

**Materials Needed:**
• Several sheets of sturdy, unlined paper, at
least 8½ by 11 inches
• A paintbrush
• Nontoxic paint *or* washable ink, thicker rather
than watery
• A container for the paint or ink

**1** Fold a sheet of paper in half,
either way, then spread it open.

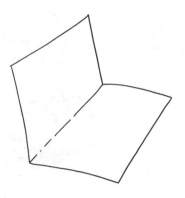

**2** With the brush, make a few dots,
twirls, lines—whatever—on *one* half of
the paper. Be generous with the paint, but
don't use so much that it will spread over
the entire surface in
step 3.

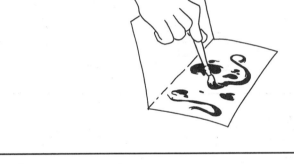

**3** Fold the sheet closed, then
press gently to spread the paint
evenly on both sides.

**4** Open up to see a double image.

## Variations:

Instead of brushing on paint, splatter droplets; try
using more than one color; try splattering paint on
*both* halves, then closing and pressing together.

# Monoprint

**Type of Activity:** Paper printing
**Object:** Make a design or drawing against a misty background
**Ages:** 10 and older

**Materials Needed:**
- Thick, nonfragile paper (better-quality printer paper is OK)
- A pen *or* sharp pencil and another pencil with a dull tip
- Nontoxic paint *or* washable ink, thick, not watery
- A large paintbrush
- An old cookie sheet (*or* old cutting board *or* plastic place mat)

---

**1** On the paper, draw a picture or design with the pen or sharp pencil.

**2** Use your brush to spread a thin layer of paint on the cookie sheet. Use just one color, or you can use several on different sections of the sheet. Make the layer good and wet but not a puddle.

**3** Press the back side of your drawing gently onto the paint. With your dull pencil, trace your drawing, pressing down firmly. Make sure to cover every line.

**4** Turn the paper over and there's your print!

# Dip-and-Dye Paper

**Type of Activity:** Paper printing the tie-dye way

**Object:** Create decorative paper for gift wrap, for party napkins, or just for fun

**Ages:** 7 and older

**Materials Needed:**
- Squares (about 8 by 8 inches) of absorbent paper (rice paper is good), paper towels, *or* napkins
- Several colors of paint *or* food coloring, fairly watery but still with distinct colors
- Several shallow bowls for the paint or food coloring
- Newspaper *or* a clothesline and clothespins

**1** Fold your paper in half once (A) and then again (B). Next, fold one corner down, forming a triangle (C), then fold the paper over into a second triangle (D). Press the creases hard.

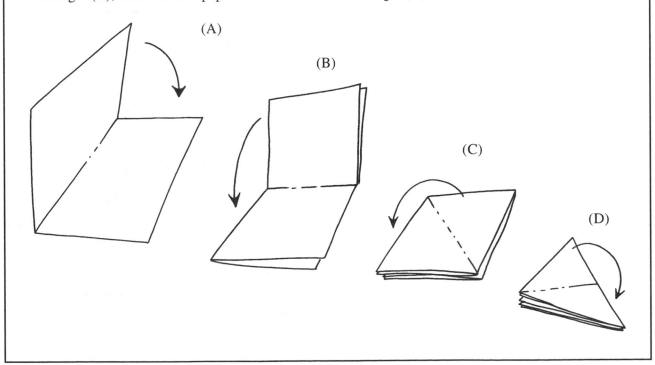

(A)

(B)

(C)

(D)

**2** Now dip each corner of the triangle into the paint. Don't leave it in long enough to seep into the whole paper.

**3** Unfold and check out the pattern! Hang your design or spread it on newspapers to dry.

## Variation:

Try other ways of folding the paper down into a small pad—for instance, in step 1 for the third and fourth folds, instead of folding to a triangle, repeat first two folds to end up with a smaller square.

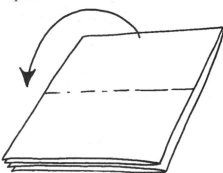
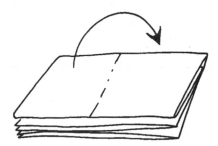

# Marvelous Marbleizing

**Type of Activity:** Paper printing with oil and water

**Object:** Create decorative paper for gift wrap, for book covers, or just for fun

**Ages:** 10 and older

**Materials Needed:**
- A deep, rectangular baking dish *or* plastic tub
- Water
- Turpentine
- Oil paints
- Mixing container(s)
- A variety of "sticks"—old chopsticks, toothpicks, a fork
- Sturdy, nonabsorbent paper (brown-paper grocery bags are good), cut to fit your tub
- Newspaper

**1** Fill the tub 3 to 4 inches deep with cool water.

**2** In your mixing container, mix turpentine with oil paint until the mixture is like thick cream. With a stick, shake drops of the paint into the water. The color should spread a little but stay on the surface. If the paint is too thick it sinks, too thin and it spreads out completely.

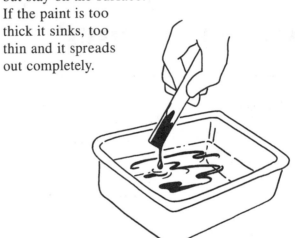

**3** Use another stick to twirl the paint into a pattern on top of the water. Don't stir too much—you'll lose the distinct shapes and color changes that make marbleized paper so attractive.

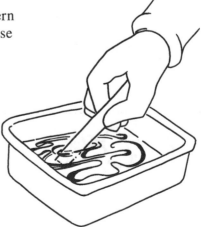

**4** Hold a sheet of nonabsorbent paper by opposite corners. Lower it onto the oil/water surface, then lift it up, turn it over, and lay it wet-side up on newspaper to dry. Keep marbleizing as long as the result is good. When you've taken up most of the paint, discard the water and start over.

**Hints:**
• Try small drops of paint or bigger ones for different effects.
• Use one color at a time or more than one.
• Stir with different sticks to create different effects.

# Sturdy Stencil

**Type of Activity:** Paper cutting and painting
**Object:** Create a stencil to use over and over
**Ages:** 9 and older—*Adult Supervision*

**Materials Needed:**
• Lightweight cardboard
• A marker *or* pen
• Paraffin (a candle *or* block of wax)
• An iron
• Scissors *or* a utility knife
• Paint and a paintbrush, *or* spray paint
• Construction paper *or* other sturdy paper
• Removable tape

**1** Draw a design on the cardboard, then rub the candle or block of wax over it, covering the picture with a thin layer of wax.

**2** With a warm iron, melt the wax into the cardboard. Let it cool completely.

**3** Cut out and remove the design, leaving the cardboard stencil. Use tape loops on the reverse of the stencil to fasten it to the paper. With the brush or spray paint, smoothly paint the area exposed by the stencil.

**4** Then lift off the cardboard. The wax repels paint—that's why you'll be able to use this stencil over and over.

# Screen Stencil

**Type of Activity:** Stenciling the silk-screen way
**Object:** Create a stencil screen to use over and over
**Ages:** 9 and older

**Materials Needed:**
- Slick paper—an old magazine cover will do
- A pencil
- Scissors
- Construction paper
- Cloth such as cheesecloth
- Small embroidery hoops
- Thick water-based (acrylic *or* poster) paint
- A container for the paint
- A squeegee *or* a wedge of thick corrugated cardboard, bent

**1** Draw a design on the slick paper, then cut it out.

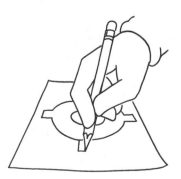

**2** Lay the cutout design on top of the construction paper.

**3** Cut a section of cloth to fit the embroidery hoops and fix the cloth snugly in the hoops. Lay the hoops—cloth down—on top of the design.

**4** Spread some paint on the cloth. With the cloth pressed against the design and construction paper, use the squeegee to spread the paint back and forth across (and through) the cloth.

**5** The paint seeps through only the holes of the design and the borders. Pull up the cloth; the stencil will now stick to the cloth, and the design is printed on the construction paper.

**Hint:** Use the design over and over until you wear out the paper. Then rinse out the cloth; when it's dry you can use it again for a different design.

# Old-Fashioned "Photo" Copy

**Materials Needed:**
- Several sheets of white paper
- Paraffin (a candle *or* block wax)
- Sunday *or* other comics *or* colored pictures in a magazine
- A wooden spoon

**Type of Activity:** Making picture-transfer paper

**Object:** Make copies of your favorite comics or other colored pictures

**Ages:** 8 and older

**1** Rub wax all over one side of the paper.

**2** Lay the paper wax-side down on the comic or other picture you want to copy. With your knuckles or a wooden spoon, rub the back of the paper down on the comics.

**3** The picture is transferred to the waxy surface—but it's backward!

**4** Press the wax picture down on a fresh sheet of white paper. Rub, and the comic appears on the clean paper—forward.

## Variation:

Transfer bits and pieces of comics, magazine pictures, and newspaper photos to a poster board to create a personal collage of images.

# Paint-Free Seascape

**Type of Activity:** Collage art
**Object:** Create a picture of the sea with no paint
**Ages:** 8 and older

**Materials Needed:**
- White glue
- Water
- A mixing bowl
- A spoon
- Tissue paper in various colors (see step 2)
- Rectangular poster board *or* sturdy cardboard
- A brush
- Scissors

**1** In the bowl, mix glue with water until it's very watery.

**2** Tear the tissue paper into long, irregular strips. For a seascape, use blues and light greens; for a landscape, blues plus tans, browns, and darker greens.

**3** Lay the poster board flat, and begin arranging the strips. Fill the whole background. A seascape might start at the bottom with tan (the sand), then many shades of blue layered up to the horizon, leaving some white background showing to suggest breaking waves. The top could be white and yellow for sky.

**4** When you like your arrangement, begin brushing the glue mixture onto the poster board. Glue the strips down one by one.

**5** Add more glue on top until the edges of the tissue strips bleed together and the colors run. It's OK if the tissue hangs raggedly off the sides—you can trim it when you're finished. You may flatten your strips completely with your glue brush, or leave them more textured.

**Hint:** Before you start arranging strips, look at some paintings or photographs of landscapes and seascapes that you like. Keep them near-by to use as guides.

# Tricky Tree Art

**Type of Activity:** Shortcut painting of a landscape
**Object:** Quickly create an expressionistic painting of trees
**Ages:** 8 and older

**Materials Needed:**
- A clean sponge—a natural sponge works best, but a synthetic one will do
- Water
- Thick watercolor paper
- Masking tape
- Poster paints *or* watercolors
- Small dishes *or* bowls, one for each color, and a bowl for the water
- An eyedropper *or* a small spoon
- A soda straw
- An old toothbrush (for Variation)

**1** Wet your sponge and use it to dampen both sides of a sheet of paper. Keep the edges of the paper dry.

**2** Tape (or weight) the paper down by the edges so it won't curl as it dries.

**3** Put some blue paint into a small dish and thin it with water. When the paper is dry, use the sponge to dab the watery paint onto the entire surface of it. This is the sky background.

**4** Dilute some black or dark brown paint. With an eyedropper or small spoon, drop some paint onto the bottom edge of the paper.

**5** Using the straw, carefully blow the dark paint up into the blue background, forming first thick lines of paint (the trunks), then thinner ones (the limbs and twigs). It may take a little practice, but you will arrive at the right effect and end up with a silhouette of trees against the sky.

## Variation:

Dip an old toothbrush into green paint, and use your thumb to flick the paint onto the trees to form sprays of leaves.

# Moonscape

**Type of Activity:** Drawing and painting
**Object:** Create a nighttime scene
**Ages:** 8 and older

**Materials Needed:**
• Sturdy paper
• Bright *or* fluorescent crayons
• Black or very dark blue water-based paint *or* washable ink
• A thick paintbrush

**1** With your crayons, draw a landscape or other scene. Your drawing should cover most of the surface of the page. Press down hard and get the crayon marks nice and thick.

**2** With the brush, paint over the entire surface of your drawing with dark paint. The paint will color only the parts of the paper not covered by crayon. When it dries, your whole picture will appear against a background of darkness.

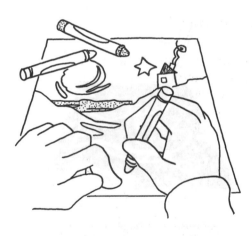

## Variation:

For a ghostly scene, use only white or white and gray crayons.

# Bleach Painting

**Materials Needed:**
- Sturdy paper
- A paintbrush
- Blue or black fountain pen ink *or* india ink
- Chlorine bleach
- Crayons, markers, *or* paint (for Variation)
- A container of water
- Rags

**Type of Activity:** Painting
**Object:** Make an interesting white-and-black painting
**Ages:** 8 and older—*Adult Supervision*

---

**1** With the brush, paint a sheet of paper with ink until the whole surface is dark. Clean your brush thoroughly by rinsing and then wiping it.

**2** When the inked paper is dry, paint a picture on the dark background with bleach. Watch as your picture slowly turns whiter and whiter.

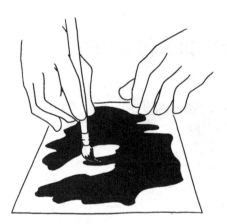

## Variation:

Once your bleach-and-ink creation is completely dry, use bright crayons, fluorescent markers, or paint to color in some of the white parts.

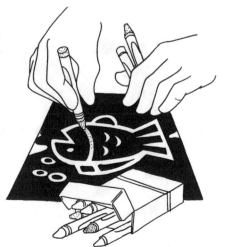

**Caution:** Bleach bleaches whatever it touches and is smelly. Do this activity in a well-ventilated area where you can't hurt furniture, carpets, or lungs.

# Photocopy Creations

Make sure, with photocopy activities, to get permission and to learn the proper way to use the copier. And please, recycle!

# Overlay

**Type of Activity:** Photocopy creation
**Object:** Use a photocopier to creatively combine images
**Ages:** 9 and older

**Materials Needed:**
- Mementos or other objects that can be photocopied (see step 1)
- A photocopy machine with the reducing and enlarging feature
- Photocopy paper for the machine
- Tape
- Scissors
- White correction fluid *or* tape
- Crayons *or* colored markers
- A dime-store frame

**1** Collect thematic materials. Let's say you and a friend visited the beach together: assemble pictures of you both, a map of the coast, a memento from your trip—a postcard, a ticket stub from the ferry. You could photocopy the map on a "light" setting, enlarged to fill the page, for the background. Make an extra copy of your background piece—whatever you choose—and set aside the "master" in case you make a mistake.

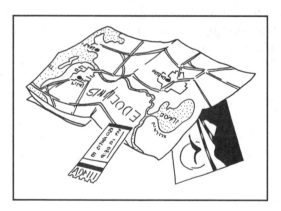

**2** Arrange your other mementos on another sheet of paper, holding them down with tape. (If using snapshots of yourselves, cut away the background.)

**3** Lay this sheet on the copier surface. Put the background sheet in the feeder or paper tray. Copy the second image onto the background.

**4** Look good? Use correction fluid for touch-ups if necessary.

**5** Make some extra copies. Hand color one, and frame it for your traveling buddy.

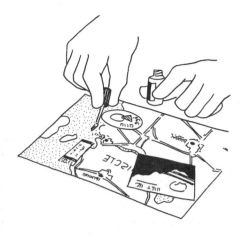

**Hint:** If your family sends newsy letters during the December holidays, you can use overlay to create special stationery for the mass mailing.

# Deco-Decals

**Type of Activity:** Photocopy creation
**Object:** Use a photocopier to create personalized decals
**Ages:** 9 and older

**Materials Needed:**
• Photocopy paper
• Pencils, pens, *or* markers (see step 1)
• Transfer type (optional)
• A photocopy machine with the reducing and enlarging feature
• Correction fluid *or* tape
• Scissors
• Clear tape
• Transparency sheets
• Clear-drying glue

**1** Create the design for your decal. If you'll be photocopying in black and white, avoid using color in your design. Use black and white pens and markers on white paper for good contrast. Draw your design in a size that's easy for you to work with; you can reduce it on the photocopier later.

**2** Transfer type will help make your letters neat, but hand printing works just as well. (Transfer type—sets of individual letters you press down onto a surface—can be bought in art stores.)

**3** Reduce your design to the desired size. Use correction fluid to make corrections. Make several copies, cut these out, and tape them onto a sheet of paper so that you get the maximum number of copies per transparency sheet. Load the copy machine tray with transparencies, and copy.

**4** Decals will glue down well to clean, dry glass, wood, luggage, mirrors, and more. (Get permission before gluing!)

## Variations:
You can also make full-color decals, but you will have to use a photocopy shop; you can buy transparency paper with a peel-off sticky back, but it doesn't stick as well as some glues.

# Flipping Out

**Materials Needed:**
- Photocopy paper
- A light pencil and an eraser
- A ruler
- A photocopy machine with the reducing and enlarging feature
- A dark marker *or* dark pencil
- Scissors
- Spray adhesive
- A small sheet of stiff paper *or* lightweight cardboard
- A stapler

**Type of Activity:** Photocopy creation
**Object:** Use a photocopier to make a flip book
**Ages:** 10 and older

---

**1** On a letter-size sheet of photocopy paper, create a 20-block grid in pencil. The grid blocks will be 2⅛ by 2⅓ inches. Draw the lines just light enough to photocopy. Make several photocopies of the grid.

**2** With a marker or dark pencil, draw (or copy) the frog and fly shown here, cut them out, and spray adhesive on the back of both. Spray adhesive is good because it lets you stick things down and pull them up many times.

**3** Attach the frog to the first block on a grid sheet, on the left side. Stick the fly down in the same block. Photocopy this page and place the resulting "master" photocopy in the feeder tray of the copier.

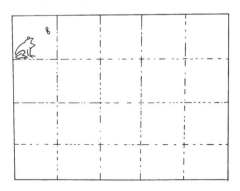

**4** Move the frog into the next block of the original grid, in exactly the same spot it was in the first block. (If you don't trust your eye, use the ruler.) Stick the fly in the block too, but very slightly closer to the frog this time. Now photocopy this version onto the master.

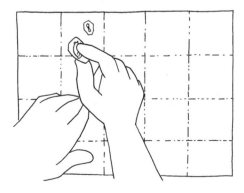

**5** Continue moving the frog and fly from block to block and photocopying it onto the same sheet. Each time, move the fly closer to the frog by a very small increment. Fill as many grids as you need until the fly reaches and enters the frog's mouth. Keep in mind that the smaller the position change of the fly in each panel, the smoother the movement will be when you flip the pages of your flip book.

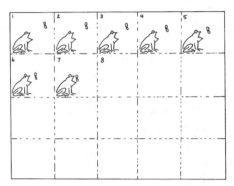

**6** "Snap" the frog's mouth shut in the final panel (omitting the fly).

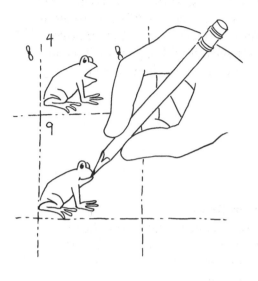

**7** Number each panel consecutively and lightly in pencil. Cut the panels out and stack them *with page 1 on the bottom.* Cut out a top cover the same size from stiff paper or cardboard, lay it on top of the small pages, and bind them by stapling. Now erase the page numbers.

**8** Flip the pages rapidly from back to front for a 2-second "moving picture."

# Variations:

### Airplane Twirl:

To form a flip book with the airplane shown here, start the plane flying level. Then in each successive panel rotate it slightly so that, during the flip of the book pages, it will appear to flip end over end and land right-side up.

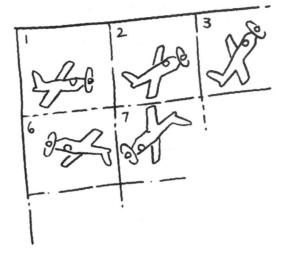

### Arrow-Head:

Cut out the head and arrow shown here. Move the arrow into one ear and out the other. You can also experiment with changing the expression on the fellow's face.

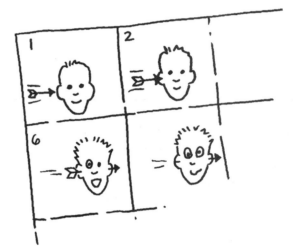

### Rocket:

The rocket moves up, arcs across the page, then disappears from sight.

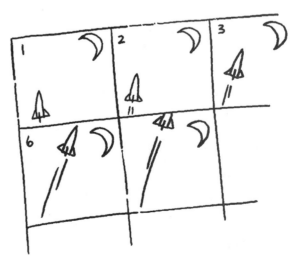

# Cut, Glue, Press, Collage, Decoupage, and Bind

# Out of Glue? Make Your Own!

**Materials Needed:**
- A mixing bowl *or* saucepan
- A stirring spoon
- Measuring cups and spoons
- Recipe ingredients
- A storage container with a lid

**Type of Activity:** Glue making
**Object:** Make your own glue for many uses
**Ages:** 8 and older—*Adult Supervision for cooking*

## #1 Basic Paste

Good for gluing paper, papier-mâché

**Ingredients:**
- 1 cup plain (not self-rising) all-purpose flour
- 1 tablespoon salt
- 1 cup water

**To Make:**
Mix the flour and salt together. Gradually add the water. Stir well until no lumps of dry flour remain. It will be thick and pasty, like cooked oatmeal. Keep the mixture in an airtight container in the refrigerator; it will last for a week or so.

## #2 Best Paper Paste

Great for gluing paper

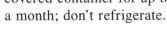

**To Make:**
In a saucepan, mix the sugar and flour together. Add the water gradually and stir all the lumps out. Simmer on the stove—don't boil—stirring constantly. When the mixture turns clear, remove the pan from the heat and stir in the oil until it is completely blended. Store the paste in a covered container for up to a month; don't refrigerate.

**Ingredients:**
- 4 tablespoons sugar
- ⅔ cup all-purpose flour
- 2 cups water
- ½ teaspoon peppermint *or* wintergreen oil

## #3 Thinner Paste

Good for more delicate paper, strip papier-mâché

**Ingredients:**
- ½ teaspoon alum powder
- ¼ cup sugar
- ¼ cup plain (not self-rising) flour
- 1¾ cups water
- ¼ teaspoon peppermint *or* wintergreen oil

**To Make:**
In a saucepan, mix together the alum, sugar, and flour. Add the water gradually, stirring out the lumps. Boil the mixture on the stove, stirring constantly. When the paste turns clear and smooth, remove the pan from the heat and mix the oil in until it is completely blended. Cover but don't refrigerate the paste; it can be stored for months.

# Puzzle It Out

**Type of Activity:** Puzzle making
**Object:** Create a simple straight-line or jigsaw puzzle
**Ages:** 8 and older

**Materials Needed:**
- A picture such as a family photo, magazine illustration, or print of a painting (avoid very thin paper, since glue might dissolve it)
- A sheet of lightweight cardboard, as large as or larger than your illustration
- White *or* mucilage glue
- Sharp scissors *or* a paper cutter
- A pencil
- A ruler

**1** Carefully glue your picture to the cardboard, smoothing out the wrinkles.

**2** Trim the excess cardboard.

**3** Using the ruler, draw a grid on your picture. Make the lines thin and light; you don't want to see them on your puzzle pieces. The smaller the pieces, the harder the puzzle will be to solve.

**4** Cut on the lines. Presto, your picture's in pieces, and you have a puzzle.

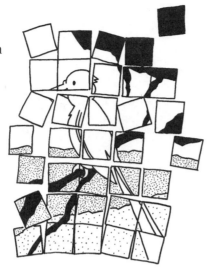

## Variation:

It's harder to cut out, but you can grid your picture in traditional jigsaw shapes. These shapes work best with puzzles that have large plain areas such as sky or sea.

# Puzzle on the Square

**Type of Activity:** Puzzle making
**Object:** Create a many-sided block puzzle
**Ages:** 10 and older

**Materials Needed:**

- Nine sheets, 7 by 9 inches or larger, of cardboard that's sturdy but that you can cut and bend
- A pencil
- A ruler
- Sharp scissors, a sharp knife, *or* a paper cutter
- White *or* mucilage glue
- Six pictures: family photos, magazine illustrations, prints, your own art. They should be 6 by 6 inches or slightly larger (avoid thin paper, since glue will dissolve it)

**1** To make the blocks, draw the pattern—according to the measurements shown here—onto the nine sheets of cardboard. It's easiest to draw and cut out one, then use it to trace the others. Cut out each one.

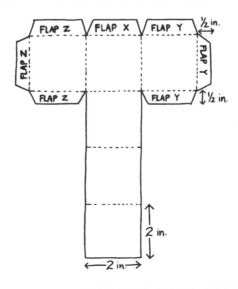

(A)　　　　　　　(B)　　　　　　　(C)

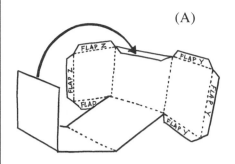
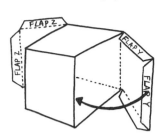
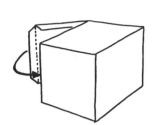

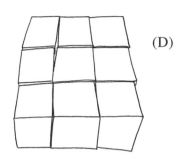

**2** To assemble a block, first crease the cardboard on the dotted lines. Fold the longest piece over, and glue it to the back of flap X (A). Put glue on the backs of the Y flaps, fold them in to finish one side (B), then repeat with the Z flaps to finish the final side (C). You will end up with nine 2-by-2-inch blocks. Arrange them in a square that measures 6 by 6 inches (D).

(D)

**3** Trim each of the six pictures to be 6 by 6 inches. Draw a 2-by-2-inch grid on each picture and cut each into nine squares. Put the squares of each picture in a pile.

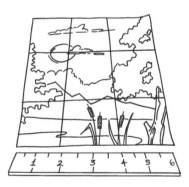

**4** Take one cardboard block, and glue one square from each of the six piles onto each of its sides. Repeat with all the blocks. You finish with a six-sided, 3-D puzzle.

**Hint:** The more similar the pieces of art (six landscapes, say), the harder the puzzle will be to solve.

## Variations:

Try any number of blocks, any shape and size of rectangle, as long as you have six pieces of art that fit; or you can buy 2-inch-thick, dense styrofoam. A carpenter with a power saw could easily cut dozens of sturdy, 2-inch-square puzzle cubes for you from the styrofoam— or from wood, for that matter.

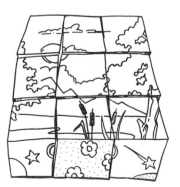

# Debris Collage

**Type of Activity:** Collage making
**Object:** Build an interesting work of art from whatever you find around the house
**Ages:** 6 and older

**Materials Needed:**
• Collage stuff: images, letters, words, patterns—whole or bits and pieces (see step 1)
• Scissors
• Any size of cardboard, poster board, *or* heavy paper for the background
• White glue, mucilage glue, *or* rubber cement

**1** Choose some neat and interesting-looking bits and pieces for your collage. Take them from: magazines, newspapers, clip art books, the Sunday comics; cereal, cookie, or other food cartons; confetti, crepe paper, wrapping paper; novelty stamps, used stamps, stamps made with your own rubber stamps; tinfoil, wax paper, party napkins, matchbooks; photographs; playing cards, baseball cards, business cards; greeting cards, seals, tinsel; construction paper, notebook paper; old calendars, postcards, brochures, invitations; and much, much more from the recycling bin, the junk drawer, the toy box. Collect related stuff for a message collage, or unrelated things that will be wild or funny when put side by side.

**2** Think about the overall effect you want to create, or the message you want to express—funny, serious, scary, or sad. Cut or tear bits and pieces of images that fit this idea. Use elements that are many different sizes to make an interesting composition.

**3** Start arranging parts on the background. When you like the arrangement you've made, begin gluing. As the look of your creation develops, you may want to go back to your box of materials for additions.

## Variation:

Start by painting your background sheet or even printing it using one of the many printing methods explained earlier in this chapter. Then build on that pattern with your collage.

# Myriad Mosaic

**Materials Needed:**
- Any size of cardboard, poster board, *or* heavy paper for the background
- A pencil
- Piles of "bits" for your mosaic (see step 2)
- White glue, mucilage glue, *or* rubber cement

**Type of Activity:** Collage making
**Object:** Arrange materials into patterns to form a picture
**Ages:** 7 and older

**1** Draw a picture or design on the background sheet. Think about colors and textures of material that will look right on different parts of the picture. For instance, on the landscape shown here, brown paper bags might work for the ground, bits of green crepe paper for the grass. You can get mosaic bits from: magazines, newspapers, notebooks, metallic paper, cellophane, construction paper, wax paper, tinfoil, wrapping paper, brown paper, rice paper, sheets of cork; toothpicks, twist ties.

**2** Cut or tear the chosen materials into bits, and arrange them in separate piles.

**3** Glue down the bits, using them like paint but clumping the same kind of bits together.

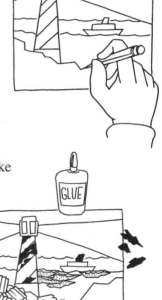

**4** Whether you cover the entire sheet or let the background show through strategically, when you finish your design it will spring to life.

## Variations:
- Shake the leftover holes from a hole puncher, or use the puncher to create circles from whatever paper you have. Make an entire collage from colored circles.
- Use a paper cutter to cut many small squares or diamonds for a roman-style mosaic.
- Use different-colored paints or markers to color a sheet of blank address labels, and cut these into self-sticking bits.

# Decoupage Flowerpot

**Type of Activity:** Paper cutting and gluing
**Object:** Make an attractive design by gluing down art
**Ages:** 9 and older

**Materials Needed:**
• Pictures or designs made by you *or* found and clipped out (see step 1)
• A clay flowerpot
• Acrylic paint
• A paintbrush
• Newspaper
• Decoupage sealer *or* plastic spray
• Scissors
• White carpenter's glue
• Wax paper
• A brayer *or* rolling pin (optional)
• A damp rag *or* sponge
• Decoupage water-base finish

**1** Choose attractive designs that will fit on the flowerpot. Draw or paint a picture yourself, or take art from magazines, Sunday comics, food packages, photos, playing cards, baseball cards, greeting cards, postcards, old calendars, brochures— look around and be creative. Shown here: putting desert images on a pot for a cactus.

**2** First, paint the flowerpot. Give it two coats if necessary, and let it dry.

**3** Lay your decorative pictures face-up on the newspaper. Spray them with sealer, let them dry, and spray them again.

**4** Cut your pictures neatly around the edges.

**5** Spread glue on the back of each picture, covering the entire surface. Stick your designs onto the flowerpot; overlapping them is OK. Lay wax paper over them and press. It is important to fix them down firmly. Rolling with a brayer or rolling pin helps, as does an extra pair of hands. Use the damp rag to remove any excess glue.

**6** Apply an even coat of decoupage finish. Allow the pot to dry for at least half an hour, and then spray and let it dry three more times.

## Variations:

You can decoupage onto many surfaces—wood, cardboard, plastic, and more. Use decoupage to decorate many, many kinds of objects:

• Paint and decoupage a cigar box.
• Decoupage large items; for instance, a footlocker or waste can. (If the surface looks OK, you needn't paint it first.) Cover most of the surface with decoupage pictures—fish for a bathroom waste can, toys for a toy box, and so on.
• Decoupage small things, such as a kitchen matchbox.
• Decoupage a thin piece of board to create a hanging picture.
• Decoupage your school notebook or an address book.
• Use decoupage to make a pencil holder out of a can or oatmeal canister.

# Japanese Screen Photo Frame

**Type of Activity:** Cutting and pasting
**Object:** Create a special frame (a great gift) for special photos
**Ages:** 8 and older

**Materials Needed:**
- Two rectangular sheets of thin poster board *or* thin cardboard, about 9 by 12 inches
- A ruler
- A pencil
- Scissors
- Four or more special photos
- Tape
- Glue
- Decorative tape
- Colored markers

**1** Fold your poster boards three times, as shown. Use the ruler to make the folds evenly spaced and straight. The boards should fit together nicely and stand up without being rickety.

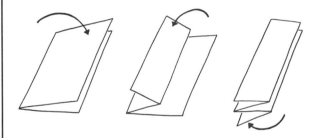

**2** On one poster board, draw and cut out "windows" for your photographs. Cut a window for each photo you want to mount. Make the windows any shape—just make sure that the openings aren't larger than your photos.

**3** Tape your photos onto one side of the board so the faces show through the windows.

**4** Glue the second poster board onto the back of the first.

**5** Finish the edges with decorative tape.

**6** Spread the screen out on the table, and decorate it with your markers. This'll be a great gift.

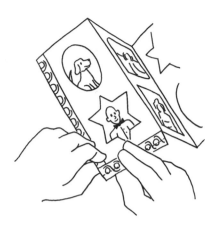

## Variations:

• Before folding and cutting your board, you can decorate it in many ways: cover it with wallpaper or wrapping paper; print on it using one of the printing methods explained in this chapter; or decorate the screen using the collage, mosaic, or decoupage techniques.

• Make the screen with as few as two panels or many, many more than the four shown here.

• Make photo windows on both pieces of poster board so that you see friendly faces from both sides of the screen.

# Super Simple Stained Glass

**Type of Activity:** Paper cutting and gluing

**Object:** Make beautiful "stained glass" from paper

**Ages:** 7 and older

**Materials Needed:**
- Heavy black, brown, or dark blue paper
- A white or yellow pencil
- Scissors
- Colored tissue paper (the more colors, the better)
- White glue

**1** With the light-colored pencil, draw a design on your dark paper that has parts that can be cut out.

**2** Cut out the "holes" of your design. What's left is your frame. Cut pieces of tissue to fit the holes.

**3** Glue the tissue pieces onto the back of the frame.

**4** Tape your creation to a bright window.

## Variation:

Use your cutout frame as a stencil to draw an exact copy of your frame on the same kind of paper. Cut out the second frame and glue it onto the back of the first (after the tissue has been glued down). Your stained glass will be tidy on both sides, and you can suspend it from a thread in front of the window, or make many small pieces and combine them in a mobile!

# Wild Weave

**Type of Activity:** Paper cutting and weaving
**Object:** Create a brightly colored wall hanging
**Ages:** 7 and older

**Materials Needed:**
• A large (12-by-22-inches or so) sheet of construction paper *or* other sturdy paper and several other sheets the same width in a different color or in assorted colors
• A pencil
• A ruler
• Scissors
• Glue
• A thin plastic or wooden dowel *or* a small straight stick from a tree
• 15-to-20-inch length of string *or* yarn

**1** Fold the large sheet of paper in half so it is approximately 12 by 11 inches. Starting at the fold, use the pencil and ruler to draw 11 lines on the paper, spaced 1 inch apart. Stop the lines 2 inches from the sides of the paper. Cut each line through the double thickness.

**2** Using the other-colored paper, draw, then cut out, 14 strips, each 12 inches long and 1 inch wide. Use one color or many colors.

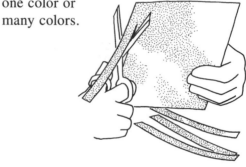

**3** Open the large sheet of paper you "sliced" in step 1 and flatten it at the fold. One by one, weave the colored strips into the large sheet as shown. (On a scrap of paper, test your glue to make sure it does not bleed through the paper.) Glue each strip neatly at each end, not letting the glue show.

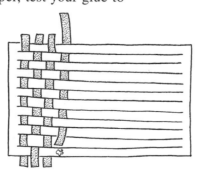

**4** When all the strips are glued, snip the bottom edge of the sheet into a fringe.

**5** Fold the top of the paper over and glue it down, leaving an opening for your dowel or stick.

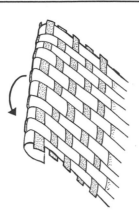

**6** When the glue is dry, slip the dowel in through the bent-over edge, then tie the string to each end of the dowel. Ready to hang!

**Hint:** In step 3, if you use several colors for your weaving strips, you can either weave the colors in randomly or, for a different look, weave them in a pattern—for instance: yellow-blue-red-purple; yellow-blue-red-purple.

# Perfect Paper Press

**Type of Activity:** Pressing and cutting paper
**Object:** Make an attractive embossed design for a greeting card or other use
**Ages:** 10 and older—*Adult Supervision*

**Materials Needed:**
- A small piece of sturdy poster board
- A pencil
- Watercolor *or* similar paper
- Scissors
- Utility knife *or* single-edge blades (optional)
- Two small scrap wooden boards
- A moist sponge
- Four C-clamps *or* heavy weights

**1** Draw a design on the poster board; size it to fit in the center of your paper. Then cut the design out. Designs with cutout parts are most attractive. For the moon shown here, use the knife to cut out the eyes and mouth.

**2** Lay the watercolor paper on one of the wooden boards. With the moist sponge, dampen the paper until it's fairly wet. Lay the poster board cutout on top of it.

**3** Lay the other board on top of this design.

**4** Have someone hold this board sandwich while you screw a C-clamp onto each side.

**5** Or, put some heavy weights on top of the boards.

**6** Let the paper dry (overnight should do it). Open the sandwich and lift the paper off the board. Here's your embossed design!

## Variation:

Cut a sheet of watercolor paper that, when folded once, will fit nicely into an envelope of your choice. Put your embossed design on one side of the fold, and you've got a unique greeting card.

# Your Own Quick Booklet

**Type of Activity:** Paper and cardboard cutting and assembling
**Object:** Make your own 8½-by-11-inch booklet
**Ages:** 10 and older—*Adult Supervision*

**Materials Needed:**
- 11-by-17-inch photocopy paper
- A 12 -by-18-inch sheet of lightweight cardboard
- Large binder-type paperclips
- A scrap wooden board
- A pencil
- A ruler
- A hammer
- Small nails
- A large sewing needle
- Embroidery thread
- A utility knife *or* single-edge blade

**1** Stack your large pages of photocopy paper. If you want a 20-page book, stack 10 pages; for a 30-page book, stack 15. Fold them in the middle to form 8½-by-11-inch leaves.

**2** Fold your cardboard sheet in the middle too, then center the pages on top of it. With the binder clips, secure the pages and the cardboard cover.

**3** Lay the spine of your book (pages up) on the wooden board. With the pencil and ruler, make a dot every half-inch down the center of the top page (total of 21 dots). Then make small holes where the dots are by lightly hammering a nail into each one, then pulling it out. Make sure the nail goes through all the pages.

**4** Thread the needle with a nice long piece of embroidery thread (about 30 inches). Count over to the 11th hole. Starting from there, stitch out to the edge. Make sure to leave a long tail hanging out. At the last hole in the paper, turn the book over and thread the entire spine on the outside.

**5** When you've finished the outside spine, turn the book back over and continue threading until you come back where you started. Tie the two ends securely. Your book is done—decorate the cover however you like. (And be sure to check out the Quick Cloth Cover, explained next.)

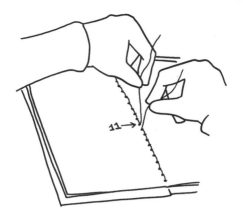

**Hint:** If your book is more than 20 pages, you may notice that the edges bulge outward when folded. After sewing, use the ruler and utility knife to trim the excess.

# Quick Cloth Cover

**Type of Activity:** Cutting, gluing, and assembling
**Object:** Make a cover for your Quick Booklet
        (see the preceding activity)
**Ages:** 10 and older

**Materials Needed:**
• Cloth (see step 1)
• Scissors
• A ruler
• A pencil
• Glue
• Cloth tape

**1** Cut a piece of cloth 1½ inches wider and 1½ inches longer than the size of your Quick Booklet cardboard cover. Use simple cotton, not a silky or stretchy fabric.

**2** Cut the piece in half so that you have one piece for each side of the spine of the cover.

**3** Draw the spine-line down the middle of the cardboard.

**4** Spread a light, even coat of glue on one half of the cardboard. Very carefully lay the cloth on it, smoothing it from the spine out. Repeat on the other half. Leave a gap of about inch between the two pieces of cloth at the spine.

**5** On the inside of the covers, fold and glue down the cloth edges, folding the corners neatly.

**6** Fold the cardboard at the spine, and sew in the pages as shown for the Quick Booklet.

**7** Use the cloth tape to cover the spine.

## Variations 1 and 2:

This cloth also works great for double-cover books, like the Snappy Scrapbook on the next page.

**1** For this version, cut two pieces of cloth, one each for the front and back covers. Make the cloths large enough to extend ¾ inch beyond the edge of the cardboard on each side.

**2** Cover both halves separately, and fold the cloth edges over on each side before binding the book.

# Snappy Scrapbook

**Type of Activity:** Paper and cardboard cutting and assembling

**Object:** Make your own 8½-by-11-inch scrapbook

**Ages:** 9 and older

## Materials Needed:
- 8½-by-11 inch paper (See step 1)
- Two 9-by-11½-inch sheets of fairly stiff cardboard
- A pencil
- A ruler
- Large binder-type paper clips
- A scrap wooden board
- A hammer
- Nails
- *Either* a yard of twine, yarn, or shoelaces and a large hairpin or bent wire; *or* brass fasteners; *or* a heavy-duty stapler (see step 5)

**1** Choose sturdy paper that can stand up to glue or tape, such as thick construction paper or watercolor paper. Neatly stack as many sheets as you would like to have in your scrapbook.

**2** On one of the cardboard sheets, draw a line from top to bottom along one of the 9-inch sides, approximately 1¼ inches from the edge. Use your ruler to make a deep crease here. This is the top cover.

**3** Lay your pages on top of your second sheet of cardboard, and place the cover on top of the pages. Secure them as shown with binder clips.

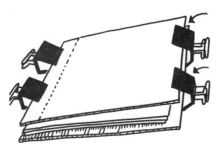

**4** Mark the 1¼-inch binding edge with five dots (one every 1½ inches). Put the scrap board under the spine, and hammer a nail all the way through each dot to make a small opening.

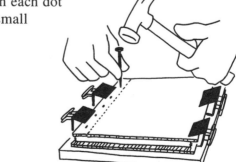

**5** Fasten the binding in one of the following ways:
- Thread your spine as shown, using the hairpin or wire as the needle.
- Use brass fasteners.
- Don't punch holes; use a heavy-duty stapler instead.

# II. 3-D Art and More

## Paper Folding— Origami and More

# Five Origami Figures

**Materials Needed:**
- Squares of lightweight paper, such as photocopy or wrapping paper (see Hint)
- Scissors
- Colored markers (if you want to decorate your sculpture)

**Type of Activity:** Paper folding and cutting
**Object:** Make a three-dimensional object from a simple slip of paper
**Ages:** 9 and older

**Hint:** If you use standard-size printer or photocopy paper, you can trim the sheets to 8½-by-8½-inch square. Then, if you want to make tiny origami figures, you can divide each of those into four sheets approximately 4 inches square.

## #1 House

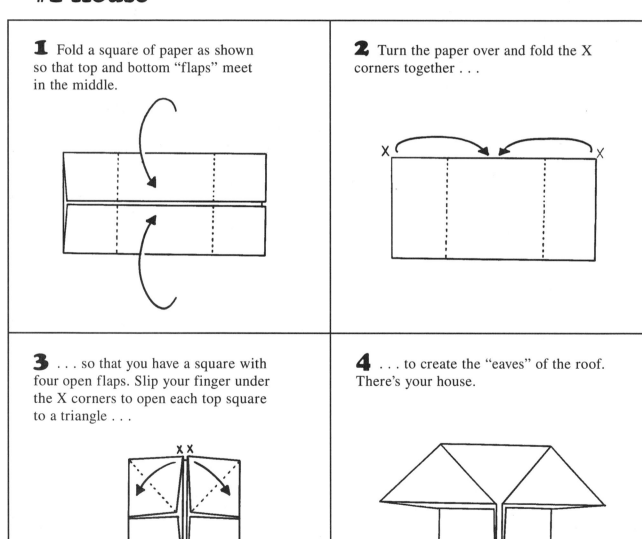

**1** Fold a square of paper as shown so that top and bottom "flaps" meet in the middle.

**2** Turn the paper over and fold the X corners together . . .

**3** . . . so that you have a square with four open flaps. Slip your finger under the X corners to open each top square to a triangle . . .

**4** . . . to create the "eaves" of the roof. There's your house.

# #2 Pig

**1** Repeat all four steps for making a house. Then, open out the flaps under the bottom two eaves of the "roof" just as you did the top flaps.

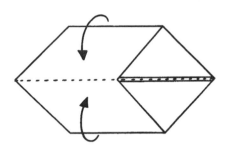

**2** Fold the Q points to meet R.

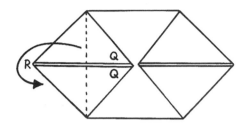

**3** Fold the paper in half as shown, then make a Z crease at both Y corners.

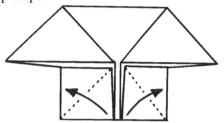

**4** Moving the Y corners forward forms the back legs of the pig.

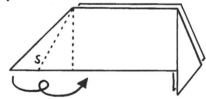

**5** Make the S creases with both outside layers.

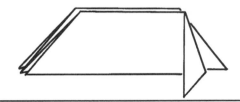

**6** Make sure to fold back only the *outer* points on the S fold, leaving the inner triangles for the pig's snout.

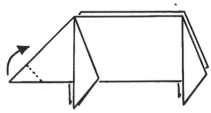

**7** Crimp the snout.

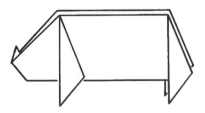

# #3 Boat

**1** Fold the paper as shown, and cut apart the Y corner along the solid line, but only to the center of the square.

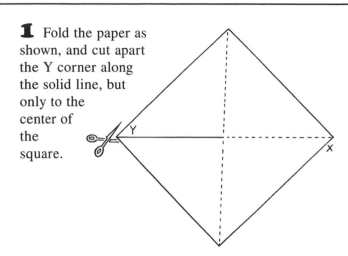

**2** Fold the paper in half so the X and Y corners come together, and make a new crease.

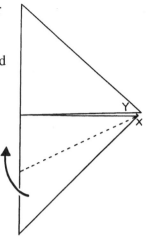

**3** Folding the bottom up at the crease gives the boat a base below its sail.

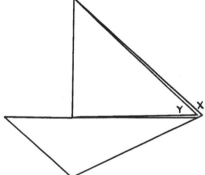

**4** Pull the Y corner away from the X corner to open the sail.

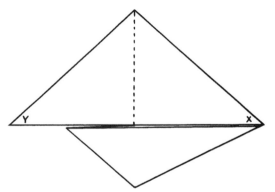

**5** Fold the sail around to the other side, the Y and X corners coming together again. Then make a crease in the bottom of the boat so it will stand.

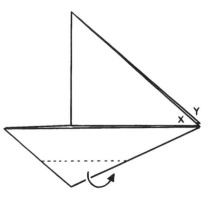

**6** Crimp the bow (front).

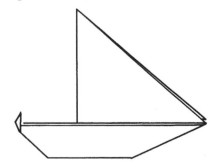

# #4 Fly

**1** Fold your paper in half to make a triangle, and make a crease about an inch from the fold.

**2** Fold one corner up on the crease, and above that crease make another crease (X) through all the layers.

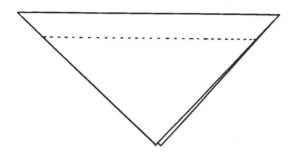

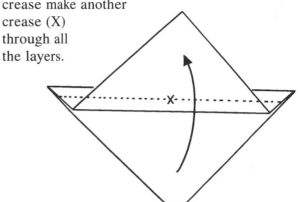

**3** Fold the second corner of the paper up at the X fold.

**4** Make the C creases as shown. Then turn the paper over to the other side.

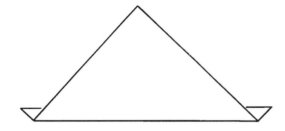

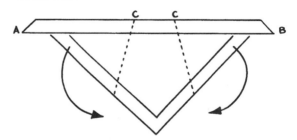

**5** Fold the A and B corners over on the C folds. Then turn the paper back to the other side.

**6** Slit Q to separate the wings. Here's the fly!

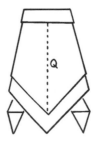

# #5 Duck

**1** Fold your paper from corner to corner (2→X) in both directions, then lay it flat. Fold lines 1→X and 3→X.

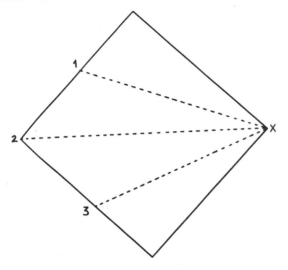

**2** Fold the flaps toward each other at lines 1→X and 3→X.

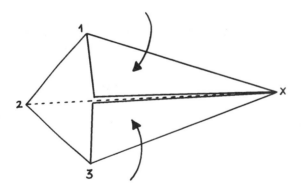

**3** Fold corner 1 down to corner 3.

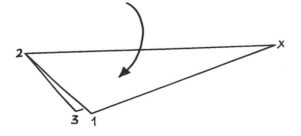

**4** Make the Y creases. Bend the paper back and forth several times on the creases.

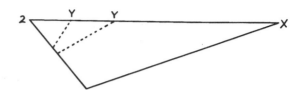

**5** Open the flaps out slightly, and use the Y creases to push the two corners inward in a "reverse fold."

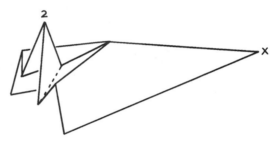

**6** Flatten the paper, and make the Z crease lines, again folding back and forth several times.

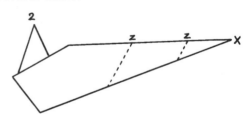

**7** Open the duck slightly again to make a reverse crease at the Z lines.

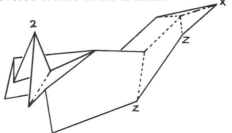

**8** Reflatten the paper.

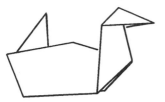

**9** Make crease lines on the belly of the bird and fold these flaps inward; these flaps let the duck stand.

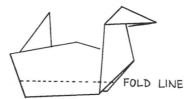

FOLD LINE

**10** And there she swims across the tabletop.

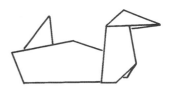

# Paper Accordion Sculpture

**Type of Activity:** Paper folding and cutting
**Object:** Make a three-dimensional wall hanging from a sheet of paper
**Ages:** 9 and older

**Materials Needed:**
- Rectangular construction paper, 8½ by 11 inches or larger
- A ruler
- A pen
- Scissors
- A cardboard strip measuring 8½ inches long (or 1 inch longer than the short side of your rectangular construction paper) and 1 inch wide
- A stapler
- A knife *or* nail
- A piece of string *or* twine, 16 or so inches long

**1** Fold a sheet of construction paper in half width-wise, then in half again.

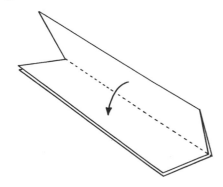

**2** Draw lines on the folded paper 1 inch apart, as shown.

**3** Cut through each of the lines on alternating sides through all the thicknesses of paper. Make sure to cut *almost* all the way to the edge, exactly as shown.

**4** Unfold the sheet and lay it flat.

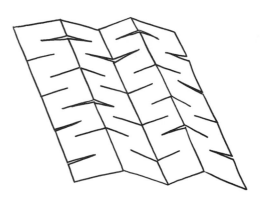

**5** Staple the cardboard strip to the topmost 1-inch strip of the paper. With the sharp point of a knife or nail, make a small hole at each end.

**6** Thread string through the holes, and knot it underneath the cardboard to secure it. Hold the sculpture up by the string, and pull gently on the bottom to open it.

# Dragon on a Stick

**Type of Activity:** Paper folding and cutting
**Object:** Make a three-dimensional object from paper
**Ages:** 9 and older

**Materials Needed:**
- A sturdy paper *or* plastic cup
- Scissors
- A hole punch, *or* a nail and board for punching holes
- A jointed drinking straw
- Tape
- A strip of construction paper approximately 2 inches wide and 17 inches long
- Glue
- Miscellaneous decorative materials (see step 5)

**1** Cut two wedges out of the cup for the jaw of the dragon.

**2** Punch two eye holes in the top of the cup and one hole underneath.

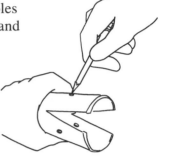

**3** Slip the straw through the lower hole up to the joint, bend it over, and tape it down inside the jaw.

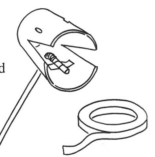

**4** Cut a curve in one end of your construction paper strip to match the bottom of the cup, and glue the paper to the cup. Fringe the tail with scissors.

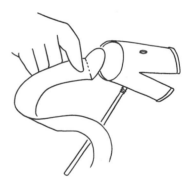

**5** Decorate! Draw scales on the body, cut a red construction-paper tongue of flame, glue button eyes on, tie ribbon streamers to the handle—the more colors the better!

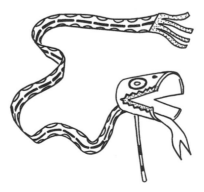

# Envelope Critter

**Materials Needed:**
- An envelope of any size
- A pencil
- Colored markers
- Scissors

**Type of Activity:** Drawing and paper cutting
**Object:** Make a three-dimensional object from an envelope
**Ages:** 5 and older

**1** Seal the flap of the envelope, turn the envelope upside down, and draw a standing-up creature on it. Draw the feet so that they don't quite reach the edge. Draw the top of the creature just touching the fold. Color your drawing.

**2** Cut out the drawing. Leave a narrow strip of blank paper attached under the feet. Keep the fold at the top intact, but slit the fold under the feet. Bend back the narrow strip of blank paper under the feet to help the figure stand up.

## Variation:
For sturdier stand-up figures, substitute a folded-over piece of lightweight cardboard for the envelope; glue a photo from a magazine (*National Geographic*, maybe?) to the envelope, then trace and cut.

# Five Fabulous Flowers

**Type of Activity:** Paper cutting and gluing
**Object:** Make a bouquet's worth of flowers from paper
**Ages:** 6 and older

## #1 Fanfold Flower

**1** Draw seven lines 1 inch apart on an 8-inch-square piece of brightly colored construction paper.

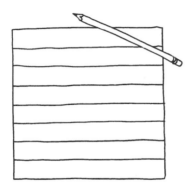

**2** Fold the paper back and forth on the lines, accordion fashion.

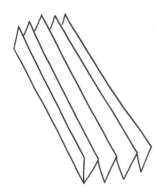

**Materials Needed:**
Note: Each individual flower uses some but not all of these materials. If you're making just one flower, do a materials checklist before beginning.
• Several colors of construction paper
• A pencil *or* pen
• A ruler
• Drinking straws
• A stapler
• Scissors
• Newspaper
• A paintbrush
• Paint
• Glue
• Cotton balls
• Several colors of tissue paper
• Green cloth adhesive tape
• A clothespin
• Pipe cleaners *or* green florist's wire
• Stems—the Flower Stems section that follows gives a number of ways to make stems; it's a good idea to select an appropriate stem style for your flower when you begin, since in some cases you'll need to make the stem first.

**3** Bend and crease the folded paper in the middle.

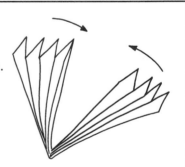

**4** Staple it to a drinking straw. Fluff it open. Cut leaves from green construction paper, and staple them to the lower part of the straw.

## #2 Fringe Flower

**1** Cut four circles out of newspaper measuring 5, 6, 7, and 8 inches across their diameters.

**2** Paint each circle, back and front. Paint the 5- and 7-inch circles the same color (for example, orange) and the 6- and 8-inch circles another color (yellow).

**3** When the paint is dry, snip the edges of each circle to create petals. Use your pencil or pen to curl the fringed edges.

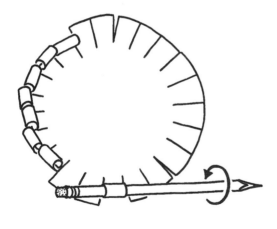

**4** Glue the circles one on top of another, with the largest circle at the bottom and the smallest on top. For the center, glue down a cotton ball.

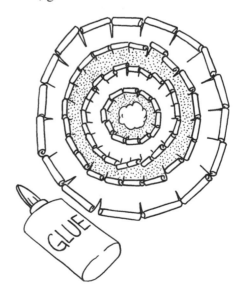

# #3 Poppy Blossom

**1** Cut five flower shapes from tissue paper. Make them all 3 to 4 inches wide. Then make a small cut in the center of each.

**2** Cut a 1-by-8-inch strip of tissue paper, using a different color from the paper you used in step 1. Make a fringe of half its width.

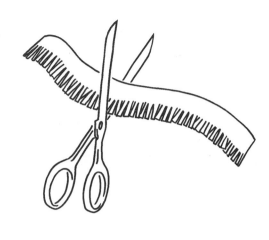

**3** Spread a light layer of glue on the unfringed edge of the 8-inch strip, and wrap and glue the strip on the end of the stem (see the following section—Flower Stems).

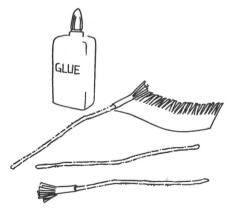

**4** One by one, push the tissue flower shapes up the stem, crimping them slightly around the fringed center. Tape the last flower shape in place on the stem with a narrow strip of green tape.

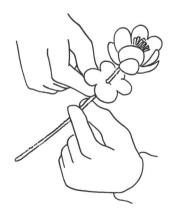

# #4  Carnation Construction

**1** Cut a long, narrow rectangle of newspaper (about 4 inches wide and 10 to 15 inches long), and paint a nice flower color on both sides. Let it dry.

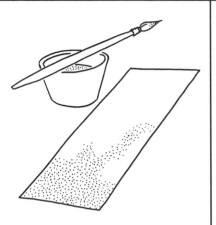

**2** Fold the paper in half lengthwise. With scissors, cut a fringe into the folded edge.

**3** Glue the edges of the strip together.

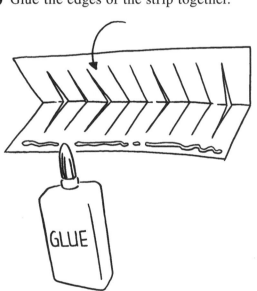

**4** Spread a light layer of glue on one side of the strip. Wrap and glue the strip tightly, fringe-side up, on the top of the stem (see the following section).

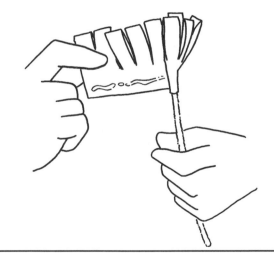

**5** Hold the pieces together with a clothespin to dry.

# #5 Twist a Bud

**1** Cut four pieces of tissue paper (one color or several) measuring 3, 4, 5, and 6 inches square. Scallop the edges of each.

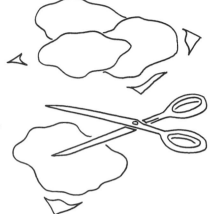

**2** Lay them on top of each other, the larger ones on the bottom.

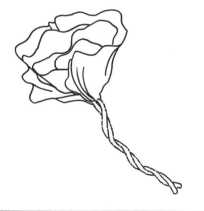

**3** Snip two holes through the centers.

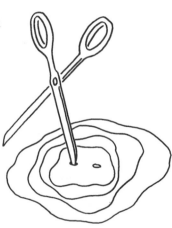

**4** Slip a pipe cleaner (or wrapped wire from the Flower Stems section) up through one hole and down through the other.

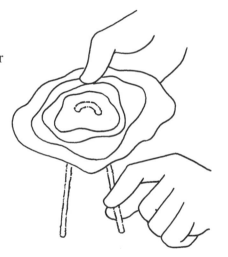

**5** Twist the pipe cleaner or wire, then gently twist and ruffle the petals.

# Five Flower Stems

**Materials Needed:**
See the individual stem descriptions.

**Type of Activity:** Cutting and assembling
**Object:** Make a variety of stems for your Fabulous
Flowers (see the previous section)
**Ages:** 6 and older

## #1 Pipe Cleaner Stem

**Material:**
• Pipe cleaners (Just use them for stems—you may paint them if you like)

**How to Attach:**
• Loop the pipe cleaner in and out of two holes, as with Twist a Bud in the preceding activity.

• Or, force the pipe cleaner through a single hole, then knot it at the top to form the flower's center.

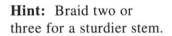

**Hint:** Braid two or three for a sturdier stem.

## #2 Newspaper Tube Stem with Leaves

**Materials:**
• Newspaper
• Glue
• A paintbrush
• Paint
• Tape

**How to Make:**
• Roll a single sheet of newspaper, any width you desire, into a tube. Spread glue on the edge, and wrap it tightly. Paint it green.

• Or, paint a sheet of newspaper green on both sides. When the paint is dry, draw a variety of leaf shapes. Cut out the leaves and glue them to the stem.

**How to Attach:**
As explained in the preceding section, you can staple, as with Fanfold Flower on page 83, tape, or glue your blossom onto the stem. You could also build your flower onto the stem, as with Carnation Construction on page 86.

# #3 Wrapped Wire Stem

**Materials:**
- Thin, stiff wire
- Wire cutters
- Green cloth adhesive *or* florist's tape
- Paint

**How to Attach:**
Same as Pipe Cleaner Stems, or use tape.

**How to make:**

**1** Cut a 6- to 10-inch length of wire. If it's too floppy, cut two or three lengths and twist them together.

**2** Wrap tape around the wire in a slightly overlapping spiral. Paint it green.

# #4 Drinking Straw Stem

**Materials:**
- Plastic or paper drinking straws
- Tape *or* glue

**How to Make:**
Just use them for stems—you may wrap them in tape, or paint them, or both.

**How to Attach:**
Straws are easy to tape or staple onto most kinds of paper flowers—and paper straws are easy to glue, too.

# #5 Natural Twig Stems

**Materials:**
- Twigs and sticks from nature
- Paint
- Glue, tape, *or* string

**How to Make:**
Simply collect these in your yard or park. You can glue on newspaper leaves (see #2—Newspaper Tube Stem with Leaves for instructions). You can also paint the sticks either natural colors or wild and metallic hues.

**How to Attach:**
Glue, tape, or tie your blossom to your twig.

# Gadgets, Toys, Music, and Jewelry

# Home-Grown Phone

**Materials Needed:**
- Two oatmeal *or* salt cartons
- A sharp object (knife, pen)
- A piece of string *or* twine, 20 or so feet long

**Type of Activity:** Cutting and assembling
**Object:** Make a low-tech telephone
**Ages:** 7 and older

**1** Remove one end of each carton. With the knife or pen, poke a small hole in the remaining end; make the hole just large enough to push your string through.

**2** Pull the string into one carton, and knot it on the inside.

**3** Do the same to the other carton.

**Hint:** To use your phone, one person whispers into one carton while a second person presses the other carton to his or her ear. For best results, keep the string stretched out and don't let it touch other objects.

# Kazoo

**Materials Needed:**
- A cardboard tube from paper towels, toilet paper, or plastic wrap
- Wax paper *or* tinfoil
- A rubber band
- A sharp pencil

**Type of Activity:** Assembly
**Object:** Make a "humdinger" of a kazoo
**Ages:** 7 and older

**1** Tear a piece of wax paper large enough to cover the tube's end with plenty of overlap. Wrap one of the ends, making sure it stretches tightly over the opening. Secure it with a rubber band.

**Hint:** To use your kazoo, press your mouth to the open end, using your hand to make a seal between your mouth and the opening of the tube. Hum or "doodle" (dum-dum-dum-dee-dee-dum-dum) your favorite song, and see how the kazoo transforms the sound.

**2** Near the wax paper fringe, use your pencil to punch one or more holes in the tube.

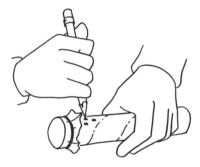

## Variations:
Use tinfoil instead of wax paper for a different sound; use different lengths of tubes for different sounds; vary the amount and pattern of the holes.

# Canned Music

**Type of Activity:** Assembly
**Object:** Make a set of bongo drums
**Ages:** 9 and older

**Materials Needed:**
- Three aluminum cans of different sizes with snap-on plastic lids, and with both ends removed (use a can opener)
- Six corks
- Glue
- Jumbo rubber bands

**1** Snap the lids onto the cans, and arrange the cans in a triangle with their open ends up.

**2** Glue two corks between each two cans. (This keeps the metal parts from ringing together when you strike the drums.)

**3** With your rubber bands, bind the three cans together at top and bottom.

**4** Flip them top up, hold them on your lap or between your knees, and drum away.

# Straw Tooters

**Materials Needed:**
- Three plastic drinking straws
- Scissors

**Type of Activity:** Cutting
**Object:** Make a set of straw "trumpets"
**Ages:** 6 and older

**1** Cut each straw into a different length. Flatten about an inch at the end of each. Crease hard so that the end stays flattened.

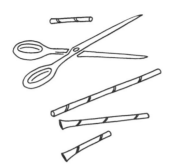

**2** Trim the flattened part of each straw into a V with your scissors.

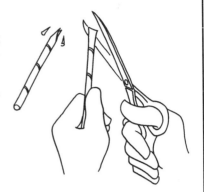

**Hint:** To use your tooters, blow into the V-shaped end, humming or "doodling" (dum-dum-dum-dee-dee) your favorite tune. Blow hard and you'll get an odd, wild-animal vibrating sound. The shorter the straw, the easier it is to blow and the higher the sound you produce.

# Paper Whistle

**Materials Needed:**
- Notebook or photocopy paper
- A pencil
- Scissors

**Type of Activity:** Paper cutting
**Object:** Make a paper whistle in a shake
**Ages:** 8 and older

**1** Draw or trace the shape shown here on paper, then cut it out.

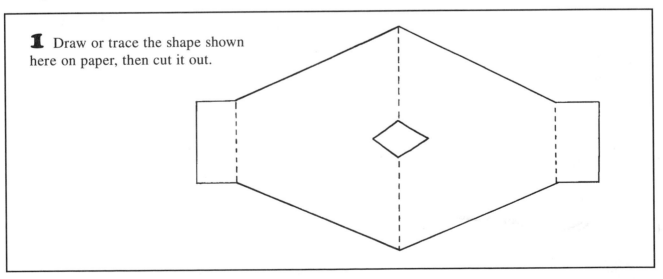

**2** Cut out the diamond in the middle, and crease the paper on the dotted lines.

**Hint:** Hold the whistle as shown, and blow into the paper between your two fingers. You can experiment with different weights of paper for different sounds, but the paper must be light enough to vibrate.

# Whirling Whistle

**Type of Activity:** Cutting and assembling
**Object:** Make a set of straw horns
**Ages:** 7 and older

**Materials Needed:**
• A piece of lightweight (not corrugated) cardboard measuring 4 by 6 inches
• A sharp pencil
• A ruler
• Scissors
• Four rubber bands (see step 2)
• A piece of string, 4 to 5 feet long

**1** Cut a rectangular hole out of the middle of the cardboard, leaving only a frame about 1 inch wide.

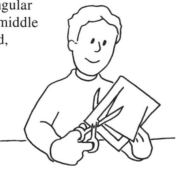

**2** Choose rubber bands that will stretch the length of the cardboard without causing it to bend. Stretch them lengthwise across the frame.

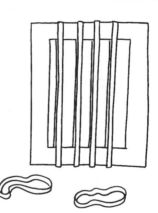

**3** Use your pencil to poke a hole in the middle of one end of the frame. Push the string through the hole, and knot it on one side.

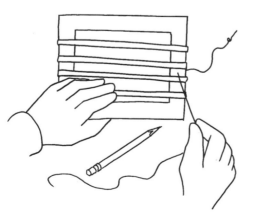

**Hint:** To use your whistle, hold it by the string, whirl it quickly in a circle around and above your head.

## Variation:
For a different sound, put a Popsicle stick (or other small stick of light wood) between the cardboard frame and the rubber bands at each end.

# Pocket Parachute

**Type of Activity:** Cutting and assembling
**Object:** Make a compact toy parachute that works
**Ages:** 7 and older

**Materials Needed:**
• A large plastic shopping bag
• A marker
• A ruler
• Scissors
• Light string, fishing wire, *or* dental floss
• A "weighty" object—a small action figure is perfect

**1** Mark out a 12-inch square on the plastic bag and cut it out. Snip a small hole in each corner.

**2** Cut four lengths of string, each 12 to 15 inches. Tie each string into one of the holes of the plastic square. Then knot the ends of the four strings together.

**3** Attach your action figure, holding the parachute as shown, and drop it from your tree house, a second-story window, or a balcony. Or, ball the whole thing up in one hand and throw it straight up as high as you can.

## Variations:
There are many ways to change the nature of the parachute's flight:

• Use shorter or longer strings.
• Cut a slit or hole in the center of the plastic square.
• Experiment with "passengers" of different weights.

# Ring and Pin

**Materials Needed:**
- A large plastic or wooden cooking spoon
- A wooden, plastic, or other ring (see step 1)
- A piece of sturdy string, 2 or so feet long

**Type of Activity:** Assembling
**Object:** Make a handheld "ring-toss" toy
**Ages:** 8 and older

**1** Choose a ring that is many times larger than the handle of the spoon. Any of these might be the right size: a curtain ring, a napkin ring, a ring sliced from a cardboard tube, a simple metal key ring. Tie one end of the string securely to your ring. Tie the other end of the string around the neck of the spoon.

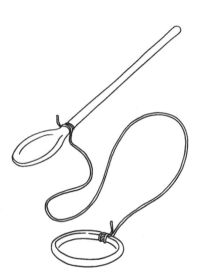

**2** To play, hold the spoon handle up, letting the string and ring hang down. Swing the ring up and try to catch it on the stick. For competitive play, whoever gets the most catches out of 10 (or 20) tries wins.

## Variation:

Tie the string around the neck of the spoon as in step 1, thread four rings onto the string, then tie the other end of the string to a fifth ring. To play, hold the spoon handle up, with the string and rings hanging down. Swing the rings up. Whoever can get them all onto the stick in the shortest amount of time wins.

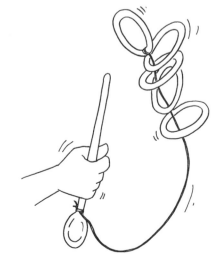

# Topsy Turvy

**Materials Needed:**
- A plastic lid from a yogurt container
- Scissors
- A coffee stirrer, pointed chopstick, swizzle stick, *or* twig whittled to a sharp point

**Type of Activity:** Cutting and assembling
**Object:** Make an instant spinning top
**Ages:** 6 and older

**1** Use the point of the scissors to make small hole in the plastic lid.

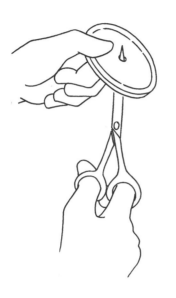

**2** Snip your coffee stirrer to make a point on one end.

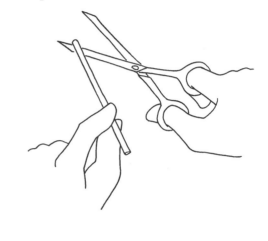

**3** Poke the stirrer or other stick through the hole.

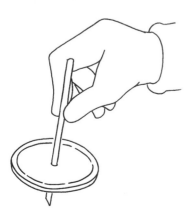

**4** Spin it between your palms!

# Milk Boat

**Type of Activity:** Cutting and assembling
**Object:** Make a pond-worthy toy boat
**Ages:** 8 and older—*Adult Supervision*

**Materials Needed:**
- A clean half-gallon (or quart) milk carton
- A pen
- A knife
- A paper or plastic plate
- Scissors

**1** Draw a line diagonally around the milk carton. Cut through the line on three sides, leaving one corner-edge intact.

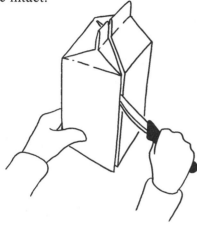

**2** Bend the carton open. Cut a slot through the middle, uncut edge.

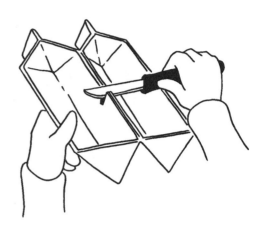

**3** Wedge the paper or plastic plate into the slot in the carton. Your boat and sail are complete.

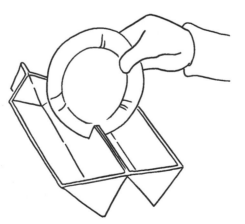

**Hint:** The wind will really catch this sail. Best to use your boat on a small pond or pool where you can run to the other side to retrieve it.

# Chinese Paper Boat

**Materials Needed:**
• A square (6 or more inches) of thick, waxed freezer paper (to make your own, see Variation).

**Type of Activity:** Paper folding
**Object:** Make an elegant boat that floats
**Ages:** 12 and older

**1** Fold your square of paper into fourths (A), then fold the two outer fourths toward the middle (B). Fold the X corners down to get . . .

(A)

(B)

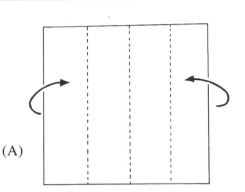
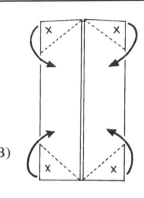

**2** . . . this shape. Fold the Y corners down to get . . .

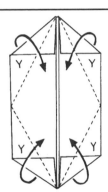

**3** . . . this shape. Fold the Z corners down to get . . .

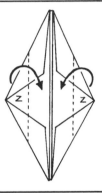

**4** . . . this shape. Now, starting with the W flaps, slowly turn the folds inside out until you end up with . . .

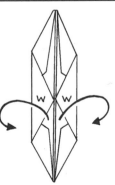

**5** . . . this shape.

**Hint:** Make all your creases nice and crisp.

## Variation:
You can make your own waterproof wax paper by rubbing paraffin onto brown paper, then ironing it to infuse the paper with wax. Allow it to dry, and you have paper that holds up very well to water. You may also drip additional wax onto the bottom and outer sides of the boat when you have completed it.

# Eye Spinner

**Materials Needed:**
- A cardboard circle 3 or so inches across
- A pencil and pens
- A piece of string about 6 inches long *or* a cut-open rubber band

**Type of Activity:** Drawing and assembling
**Object:** Create an optical illusion
**Ages:** 9 and older

**1** Draw the horse on one side of the cardboard disk and the rider on the other, as shown. Make sure you draw them so that they seem upside down to each other on their different sides.

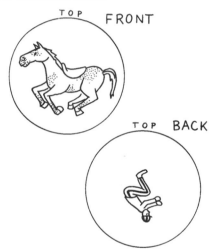

**2** Poke very small holes with your pen or pencil on each side of the cardboard (near the horse's head and tail). Push the string or rubber band through the holes.

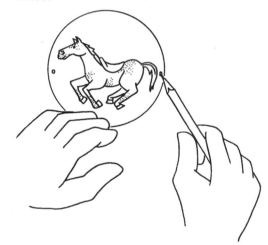

**3** Hold the ends of the string and have someone wind the cardboard disk until the string is twisted tight. Then have the person let go—as the disk twirls, the rider jumps onto the back of the horse.

## Variations:

Draw a head with hair on one side, the face on the other; draw a jack-in-the-box with the jack on one side, box on the other; draw the bars of a cage on one side, a bird on the other.

# Clown-on-a-Wire

**Materials Needed:**
- Paper
- A pencil *or* pen
- Scissors
- A ruler *or* wooden paint stirrer
- Rubber cement

**Type of Activity:** Drawing and cutting
**Object:** Make a tightrope-walking clown in just a couple of minutes
**Ages:** 8 and older

**1** Draw clown figure shown here, or a figure of your own choosing, and cut it out.

**2** Crease a strip of his shoe-bottoms back, and use the rubber cement to stick him to the ruler so he stands up.

**Hint:** To make the "tightrope" action, wiggle the ruler and the clown wobbles and bobbles and seems to lose his balance and right himself over and over again.

# Paper Gliders

**Materials Needed:**
- A rectangular sheet of paper—anything from photocopy paper to construction paper; somewhat heavier paper will make a more stable glider
- A light paper clip *or* other weight (optional)

**Type of Activity:** Paper folding
**Object:** Make a few simple gliders that really glide
**Ages:** 7 and older

## #1 Wide-Wing Flyer

**1** Fold the top quarter of the paper as shown.

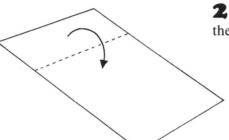

**2** Fold the paper down the middle.

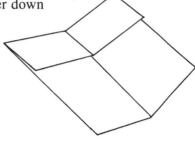

**3** Fold the top corners, and bend them to the middle.

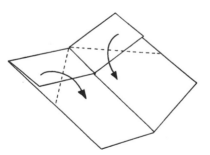

**4** Fold a nose . . .

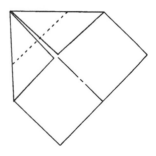

**5** . . . and fold it over.

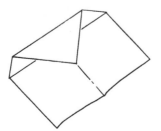

**6** Add two creases by the center crease, folding downward . . .

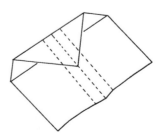

**7** . . . to create a gutter. You may add a paper clip to the nose. Try flying your craft with and without the paper clip.

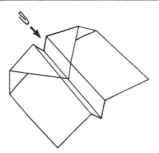

# #2 Classic Narrow Flyer

**1** Fold the sheet in half lengthwise, and crease two of the corners.

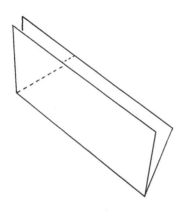

**2** Fold the two corners down so their edges line up with the bottom. Then make another lengthwise crease.

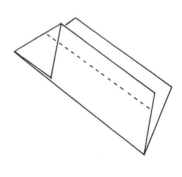

**3** Fold the creased flaps down in opposite directions—for the wings.

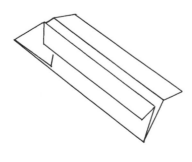

**4** It flies great.

# #3 Rocket Glider

**1** Fold the sheet in half lengthwise, and crease two of the corners.

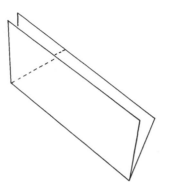

**2** Fold the two corners down so their edges line up with the bottom. Then make another crease, as shown.

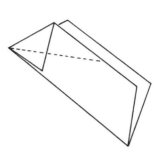

**3** Fold these creases down in opposite directions—for the wings.

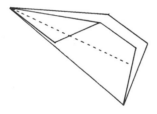

**4** Completed—it zips through the air.

# Catstep Dachshund

**Type of Activity:** Paper folding
**Object:** Make a dachshund
**Ages:** 8 and older

**Materials Needed:**
- Eight strips of construction paper at least 11 inches long and 1 to 1½ inches wide
- Tape
- Scissors
- An (approximately) 8-by-11-inch sheet of construction paper.
- An (approximately) 4-by-5-inch sheet of construction paper.
- Additional construction paper
- Colored markers

**1** To make the "catsteps," lay two of the strips of paper, corner on top of corner, at right angles to each other. Tape them together.

**2** Fold the two strips back and forth across each other. Trim off any leftover bits.

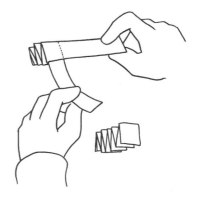

**3** Tape the top closed, then gently stretch the paper open. You now have one catstep leg; make three more.

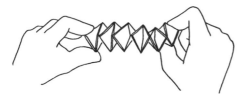

**4** Make the pup's body by rolling the 8-by-11-inch sheet of paper into a tube. Tape the seam closed, and tape the four legs you just made to the body.

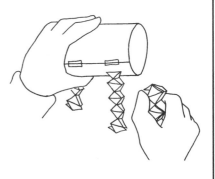

**5** Make the pup's head by rolling the 4-by-5-inch sheet of paper into a tube; tape the seam, then tape the head to the body. You can also draw in a mouth and eyes, cut ears from the extra paper, and tape them to the pup's head, and give him a tail.

## Variation:
Change the shape of the body and head and the length of the catstep to make any creature, real or imaginary.

# Catstep Marionettes

**Materials Needed:**
- Strips of construction paper at least 11 inches long and 1 to 1½ inches wide
- Tape
- Sheets of construction paper
- A pencil
- Scissors
- Glue
- A large needle
- Embroidery thread
- Straight tubes *or* sticks, 12 to 18 inches long
- Newspaper

**Type of Activity:** Paper folding and cutting
**Object:** Make a catstep snake or ostrich puppet
**Ages:** 8 and older

## # 1 Snake

**1** Tape together five or six strips of paper into one long strip. Use steps 1–3 from Catstep Dachshund (the preceding activity) to make a long catstep.

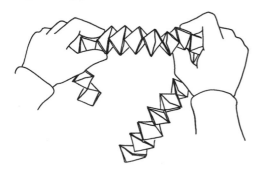

**2** Draw a forked tongue on construction paper, cut it out, and glue it to one end of the catstep.

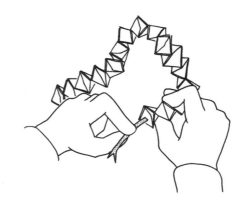

**3** Use the needle to pierce the snake in three places, and tie on three 12- to 18-inch lengths of thread. Then tie them to the stick and make him wiggle.

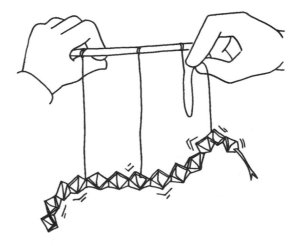

## #2 Ostrich

**1** Tape together several strips of paper to make two long (8- to 10-inch) cat-steps for the legs and one shorter catstep for the neck. (Again, follow steps 1–3 from Catstep Dachshund.)

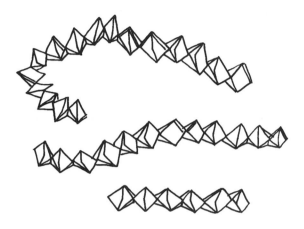

**2** Spread glue thinly and evenly over two sheets of 8-by-10-inch construction paper. Glue them together. Repeat with three more sets of two sheets, for a total of four.

**3** When the sheets are dry, draw the ostrich head and body on one, the wings and tail on another, and cut them out.

**4** Use the cutout parts to trace a second set on the other glued sheets, and cut these out. You should end up with two identical heads, two identical bodies, two sets of wings, and two tails.

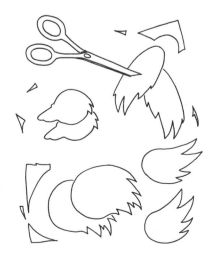

**5** Glue the body and head pieces together on the edges, leaving openings as shown.

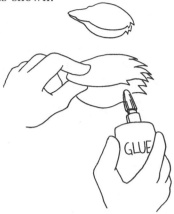

**6** Stuff the head and body with just enough wadded newspaper to give them a little shape. Then glue them closed.

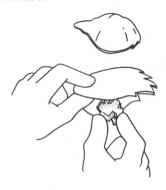

**7** Glue together the legs, neck, head, wings, and tail.

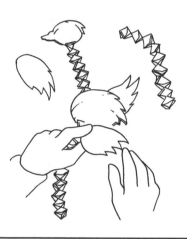

**8** Cross two tubes and tape them together.

**9** Use the needle to pierce the ostrich's body, head, and legs. Tie on four lengths of thread, and attach your ostrich to your crossed tubes. Let 'er fly.

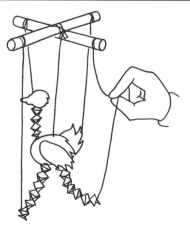

## Variations:

With this basic construction method you can make all kinds of four-legged creatures, spiders, octopuses, and whatever you can dream up.

# Magazine Bead Necklace

**Type of Activity:** Paper cutting and gluing
**Object:** Make a unique necklace
**Ages:** 8 and older

**Materials Needed:**
- Lightweight cardboard
- A pencil
- Scissors
- A ruler
- Many brightly printed magazine pages
- Glue and a small brush
- Water
- A paper or plastic cup for mixing the glue
- Thin nail *or* thick wire
- Embroidery thread and large needle

**1** For every bead you make you need a long, narrow triangle of paper. Cut out a triangle from the cardboard, measuring about 1 inch wide at the base and several inches long. Use this to trace triangles onto the entire surface of many sheets of magazine paper. Cut them all out.

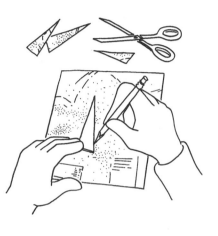

**2** Dilute white glue with a little water.

**3** To make a single bead, select one triangle and spread glue on the less interesting side, just barely to the edges. Leave a quarter-inch strip free of glue at the base of the triangle.

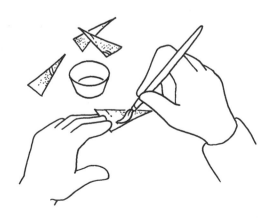

**4** Wrap the unglued part of the paper around a nail. Keep wrapping until the whole triangle is wrapped around itself, with the pointed end in the middle. Smooth the edges, gently wipe off the excess glue, slip out the nail, and let the bead dry. Make 5, 10, dozens.

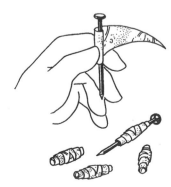

**5** String the beads together with a needle and thread. When your strand is long enough to slip over a wearer's head, tie a very secure knot.

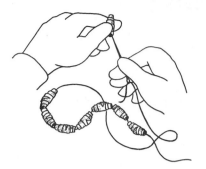

## Variation:

Make a mix-and-match necklace with other beads, such as the ones you can buy in craft stores.

# Hawaiian Lei

**Materials Needed:**
- Newspaper
- Scissors
- A ruler
- A heavy-duty needle
- Light string *or* dental floss
- Paintbrushes
- Paint

**Type of Activity:** Paper cutting and gluing
**Object:** Make an island necklace
**Ages:** 6 and older

**1** Cut a whole bunch of 12-inch squares of newspaper, and crumple them into balls.

**2** Thread them together and tie them into a loop.

**3** Paint them bright colors, like flowers.

# Sculpt!
# Dough, Plaster,
# Papier-Mâché, and More

# Make Your Own Play Dough

**Type of Activity:** Mixing
**Object:** Make reusable, nonhardening molding dough
**Ages:** 8 and older—*Adult Supervision*

**Materials Needed:**
- 1½ cups of water
- A small saucepan
- 2½ cups of plain (not self-rising) flour
- 1 cup of salt
- 1 tablespoon of alum powder
- A large mixing bowl
- A large stirring spoon
- 4 tablespoons of oil
- Food coloring
- Resealable plastic bags

**1** Boil the water in the saucepan. In the large bowl, mix together the flour, salt, and alum, then stir in the oil.

**2** Stir the boiling water into the flour mixture until it's all mixed.

**3** When the mixture is cool enough, use your hands to knead the dough until it's smooth.

**4** Divide the dough, making a separate pile for every color you'd like to make. Knead a few drops of food color into each lump.

**Hint:** Your dough will last a long time stored in a resealable plastic bag, even longer if refrigerated.

# Plaster of Paris Molding

**Materials Needed:**
- Plaster of paris and water (see step 1)
- A measuring cup
- A plaster casting mold (see step 1)
- White glue (see step 2)
- A tablespoon
- A large mixing bowl
- A large stirring spoon

**Type of Activity:** Mixing and molding
**Object:** Make hard-drying, permanent plaster molds
**Ages:** 9 and older

---

**1** Molds and plaster (powder) are sold in art and hobby stores. Normally, you mix two parts plaster to one part water (2 cups to 1 cup; 3 cups to 1½ cups; and so on). If your mold doesn't say exactly how much plaster to use, fill it with dry plaster, measure it, then place the plaster in the bowl.

**2** Measure out the water—one-half the amount of plaster. For an extra strong cast, add 1 tablespoon of glue for every ¼ cup of water.

**3** Thoroughly mix glue-and-water with the plaster. Pour the mixture into your mold. (If you find there's not enough, just make another batch.) Set it aside to harden. Plaster dries hard and smooth. It will turn out of the mold easily and also take paint well, and you can use the mold again.

**4** Many, many different kinds of molds are available.

# Speed Plaster Sculpture

**Type of Activity:** Mixing and molding
**Object:** Create a permanent plaster sculpture
**Ages:** 9 and older

**Materials Needed:**
- A frame for the sculpture (see step 1)
- Plaster of paris (see step 3)
- Water
- Alum powder
- A measuring cup
- A teaspoon
- A mixing bowl
- A stirring spoon
- Paper towels, gauze, *or* worn-out bedsheets, in strips
- Miscellaneous sculpting tools (see step 4)
- Watercolor *or* poster paints and a paintbrush (optional)

**1** Use a cardboard cone or a large bottle for the understructure. Or, form the general shape from chicken wire.

**2** Have your structure ready and the idea for your sculpture in mind before mixing the plaster. You'll have only 15 to 20 minutes to work before the plaster becomes too thick to use.

**3** Mix the plaster. Amounts will vary according to the size of your project. A general recipe is: 1½ parts plaster, 1 part water, and 1 teaspoon alum per cup of water. First mix the plaster and alum, then add water. Stir the mixture until it's smooth.

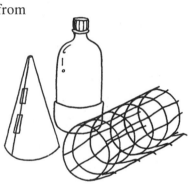

**4** Dip strips or sections of cloth into the plaster mixture. Then drape them on your understructure. Use your fingers, a stick, a spoon, or whatever is at hand to help shape your sculpture.

**5** When it's dry, you can paint it. (See Hint under Plaster Fresco, which follows.)

# Plaster Fresco

**Type of Activity:** Mixing and painting
**Object:** Paint a permanent plaster fresco
**Ages:** 9 and older

**Materials Needed:**
• A sturdy wooden picture frame
• White glue
• A piece of paneling *or* other thin wood, the same size as the frame
• Wood tacks
• A hammer
• Wall-patching plaster
• Water
• A measuring cup
• A mixing bowl
• A stirring spoon
• A small sheet of cardboard
• Watercolors *or* poster paints and a paintbrush; a stencil (optional)

**1** Put a line of glue on the back of the picture frame. Press the thin piece of wood down on top of it, and use your hammer and tacks to fasten it securely.

**2** Mix the plaster according to the package instructions. Pour the plaster into the frame. Lift the whole thing an inch or 2 above the table and drop it several times. This removes the air bubbles.

**3** Smooth the surface with the cardboard.

**4** Let the plaster dry. When it is still damp, either freehand or with a stencil, paint a picture or design.

**Hint:** Some paints react badly to plaster. To test paint, mix a little bit of it with dry plaster. If the color is still nice after a week, the paint should be OK for fresco painting.

# Lint Modeling

**Materials Needed:**
- 3 cups of dryer lint (see step 1)
- A medium-size saucepan
- 2 cups of water
- ⅔ cup of plain (not self-rising) flour
- 3 drops of wintergreen oil
- Newspaper *or* a large sheet of cardboard

**Type of Activity:** Mixing and sculpting
**Object:** Make a durable, hard-drying sculpture
**Ages:** 8 and older—*Adult Supervision*

---

**1** Lint builds up fast in home dryers. You can also collect lint from a commercial laundromat for a large project. Put the lint in the saucepan and add the water. Make sure to get the lint thoroughly wet. Mix in the flour, then add the wintergreen oil.

**2** Cook the mixture over low heat, stirring constantly. Keep stirring until it's thick enough to form peaks on the surface.

**3** Pour the mixture out onto newspaper or cardboard to cool.

**4** Use the material like modeling clay to make your object.

## Variation:

You can also fashion objects using an understructure (see step 1 of Speed Plaster Sculpture). However, with lint you don't need to work so fast. The lint mixture stays pliable for days if stored in an airtight container. It makes an interesting papier-mâché substitute.

# Papier-Mâché Recipes, Techniques, and Projects

**Type of Activity:** Mixing and sculpting
**Object:** Create a hard-drying, lightweight, durable sculpted object
**Ages:** 9 and older

**Materials Needed:**
- Plain all-purpose flour (not self-rising)
- Salt
- Water
- A large bowl
- A wooden spoon
- Dry wallpaper paste (optional)
- Newspaper
- A bucket *or* large pot
- Paint, varnish, shellac, and brushes, and any other decorative materials desired
- A dipping container
- Various molds and understructure materials for strip-and-layer projects
- Masking tape
- Wax paper

## #1  Paste recipes

### Classic Paste
Mix ½ cup flour, 1 tablespoon salt, and 1 cup warm water. The mixture should be like gravy. Sprinkle in additional flour or water to get it right.

### Wallpaper Paste
You may also buy dry wallpaper paste and mix it according to the instructions on the box. Add enough extra water, if necessary, to make it the consistency of gravy.

### Variation:
See also #1 Basic Paste on page 52.

## #2  Pulp Method

**1** Tear up many sheets of newspaper into bits 2 inches square or smaller. Press them into the bucket until you have roughly a gallon's worth. Cover the paper with water and let it sit overnight.

**2** Squeeze out the excess water from the newspaper. Then mix in 2 tablespoons of paste. The object is to get the consistency of squishy clay.

**3** Use your hands to mold this "clay" into any shape you choose, then let it dry. (Drying takes from 1 to several days.) When your project is dry, you may paint, varnish, or shellac it. It will be very hard, last virtually forever, and not break easily.

**4** Pulp is also good for adding detail to papier-mâché objects made with the Strip-and-Layer Method (#3, which follows).

## Variation:

In step 2, if you mix in 1 tablespoon paste and 1 tablespoon white glue, your sculpture will be stronger when dry. However, paste mixed with glue is a little harder to manipulate. For an even harder-drying papier-mâché, you can add a little sawdust to the pulp.

# #3 Strip-and-Layer Method

**1** Tear newspaper into strips. Depending on the project, the strips may be from 1 inch to several inches wide. Strips 5 to 10 inches long are easiest to work with. For making items such as bowls or trays, you may even use long rectangular pieces.

**2** Put the paste in a bowl large enough for you to dip strips into it. Add water to the paste if necessary to make it gravylike in consistency.

**3** Dip strips of newspaper into the paste, wetting them thoroughly. Slide the strip between two fingers to remove excess paste.

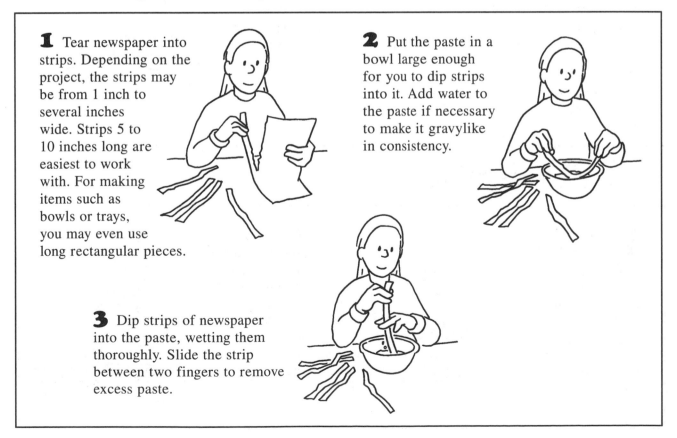

**4** Lay these strips onto a mold or understructure, layer after layer, to form the desired shape.

**5** Pulp (see #2, Pulp Method, page 120) may be used to add features.

## Make Pulp Beads

**Additional Materials Needed:**
- A long thin nail
- Wax paper
- A sturdy needle
- Strong thread

**1** Prepare pulp as explained in the section Pulp Method (page 120). Shape the pulp into balls about the size of marbles—various sizes or all the same. Make enough beads for a nice long string.

**2** Pierce the center of each bead with the nail to create an opening for stringing them.

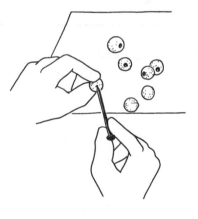

**3** Spread them on wax paper for drying.

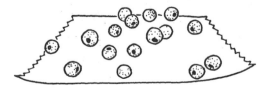

**4** When your beads are completely dry, paint them—and when the paint's dry, shellac them if you like. Let each coat dry, then string the beads and knot the string.

# Make a Snake, a Lizard, or Any Shape with Pulp

**1** Prepare pulp as explained earlier in the section Pulp Method (page 120). Shape the pulp into a snake.

**2** From the basic snake shape you can coil the body upright. Add a hood to the shape, and you have a cobra.

**3** Or, you could take a short version of your basic snake shape and add legs, and you have a lizard.

**4** Place your completed objects on wax paper to dry. Then paint, shellac, or otherwise decorate as you like.

# Make a Bangle

**Additional Materials Needed:**
- Lightweight cardboard
- A pencil
- A ruler
- Scissors
- Paper towels

**1** Cut a strip of cardboard 10 inches long and 1 inch wide. Bend it into a circle. (If the bracelet's for you, try the band on your wrist and adjust it to a size you like.) Tape it with the masking tape.

**2** Roll up and flatten a sheet (or two) of paper towel, and tape it to the outside of your cardboard circle.

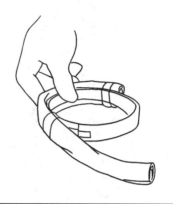

**3** Wrap the whole thing with masking tape.

**4** Dip newspaper strips into the paste, loop them around and around the tape-covered band. Cover the band with three layers.

**5** Let it dry, then paint and decorate. (Gold paint and sequins would make it extra-fancy, and so would gluing on fake jewels.)

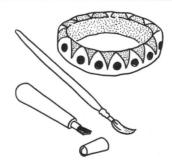

# Make a Bowl

**Additional Materials Needed:**
- Bowl to use as mold (step 1)
- Sandpaper (optional)

**1** Choose a bowl whose shape and size you like. Tear 10 or so full sheets of newspaper into long rectangular pieces. Make them large enough to stretch across the bottom of your bowl, from one side to the other.

**2** Fill a dipping container—one that that will accommodate your pieces of newspaper—with a generous amount of paste (any of the papier-mâché paste recipes in this book will do).

**3** Dip a piece into the paste, making sure to get it completely wet.

**4** Turn the bowl upside down, and lay the wet sheet across the bowl. Press the sides down smoothly.

**5** Continue with the remainder of the pieces. Lay each one across the bowl at a slightly different angle.

**6** When completely dry, the papier-mâché bowl will slip off the model bowl. Trim (or sand) the lip of the bowl, and paint it as you like.

## Variation:
You can also construct a decorative tray: Form the understructure from cardboard and masking tape. Layer the form with sheets of newspaper, let it dry, then paint and decorate.

## Make Maracas

**Additional Materials Needed:**
- Small balloons
- Scissors
- A handful of seeds *or* small beans
- Stiff, slim cardboard tubes, both ends covered with masking tape

**1** To make each maraca, blow up a balloon to the size of an orange and knot it.

**2** Cover it with four or five layers of newspaper strips dipped in papier-mâché paste, and allow it to dry. (Use any one of our paste recipes.) Leave the balloon's tail uncovered.

**3** Cut off the balloon's knot and pull out the balloon, leaving an opening about the size of the cardboard tube.

**4** Pour in the seeds.

**5** Insert a cardboard tube just slightly into the opening, and tape it securely in place with masking tape.

**6** Cover the tube with several layers of paste-dipped newspaper strips, and allow it to dry.

**7** Paint and decorate your maracas.

# Make a Jack-o'-Lantern Piñata

**Additional Materials Needed:**
- A large, inflated balloon
- Sturdy twine
- Orange tissue paper cut into 3-inch-wide strips
- Rubber cement
- Scissors
- A black marker
- Lightweight cardboard

**1** Tear a lot of 2-inch-wide newspaper strips. Dip them into papier-mâché paste and lay them onto the inflated balloon. Apply four layers, each at a different angle from the last. Leave a 2- to-3-inch-wide uncovered area.

**2** Allow the form to dry completely. Prick it to deflate the balloon inside and then remove the balloon.

**3** Fill the shell with treats.

**4** Fit the form with a harness of twine, securing it in several spots with masking tape. Leave a well-knotted hoop (for hanging) above the opening.

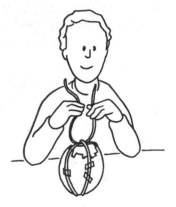

**5** Close the opening with masking tape, at the same time securing the hoop well.

**6** To make tissue ruffles:
- Fold strips of tissue in half length-wise, and glue the edges with rubber cement.
- Snip the folded edge into a fringe.
- Glue the strips in a spiral around the piñata so that the ruffle of each successive strip hides the glued edge of the last strip.

**7** Use the black marker to make facial features on cardboard. Cut them out and glue them to the piñata. Hang it from the loop, get a big stick, and go at it!

# Paper Roll Bowl

**Materials Needed:**
- A roll of paper an inch or so wide and 10 or so feet long (see step 1)
- Scissors
- A ring of cardboard about an inch wide (see step 2)
- A sheet of lightweight cardboard
- A pencil
- Tape
- White glue mixed with water
- Brushes
- Paint

**Type of Activity:** Paper and glue construction
**Object:** Create a bowl from a roll of paper
**Ages:** 7 and older

**1** You can buy adding-machine tape and either use it as is or cut it in half if it's too wide. Or, use scissors or a paper cutter to make multiple strips of paper, then overlap the ends and glue them together to create a roll. The longer the strip, the higher the sides of your bowl will be.

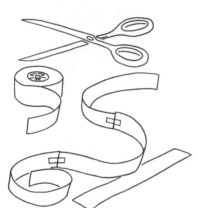

**2** For the base, you can use an empty masking-tape ring. Or make your own by curling a strip of cardboard in a circle and overlapping and gluing the edges.

**3** Cut a disk of cardboard that fits perfectly inside the circle. Tape it in place inside the circle, then brush glue on the outside rim of the circle.

**4** Glue one end of the roll of paper tape to the rim. Continue wrapping all of it around snugly.

**5** Ease the rolled paper upward in a spiral. Let each ring rise just slightly above the preceding one.

**6** Brush glue over the entire surface of the bowl. When it's dry, paint it as you like.

# Clay and Toothpick Construction

**Materials Needed:**
• Modeling clay *or* play dough
• Toothpicks

**Type of Activity:** Rod and ball building
**Object:** Have fun creating unique sculptures
**Ages:** 6 and older

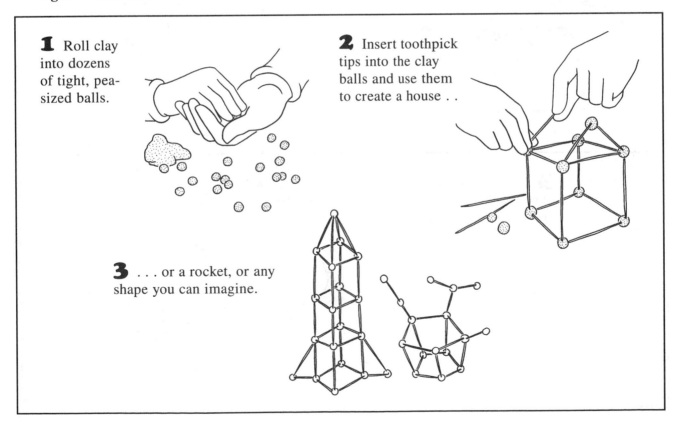

**1** Roll clay into dozens of tight, pea-sized balls.

**2** Insert toothpick tips into the clay balls and use them to create a house . . .

**3** . . . or a rocket, or any shape you can imagine.

# Soap Whittle

**Materials Needed:**
- Paper
- A pencil
- A large bar of soap
- A small paring knife

**Type of Activity:** Soft sculpting
**Object:** Sculpt the object of your choice
**Ages:** 8 and older—*Adult Supervision*

**1** Decide what you want to sculpt. Draw it first on paper, from all sides.

**2** With the knife, etch the outline of your design from all sides onto all sides of the soap, following your drawing.

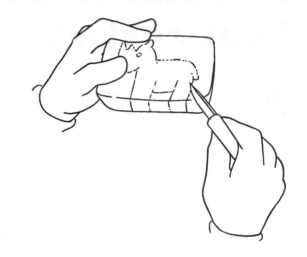

**3** Carve! Take your time, go slowly, checking all angles front and back as you proceed.

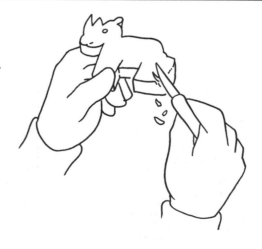

# Tin Can Lantern

**Type of Activity:** Light carpentry
**Object:** Make a candle lantern from trash
**Ages:** 9 and older—*Adult Supervision*

**Materials Needed:**
- A clean, empty food can with the label and top removed
- A permanent marker
- Water
- An old towel
- Nails
- A hammer
- Gloves
- A candle
- Long matches

**1** Mark a pattern of dots on the outside of the can.

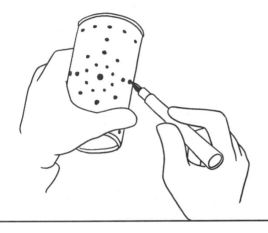

**2** Fill the can with water and set it in the freezer until the water is frozen solid.

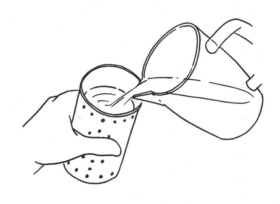

**3** Hold the can on its side, resting on the towel (it's easier to hold with gloves). Carefully pierce each dot with the hammer and a nail. Drive the nail in just far enough to make a small hole.

**4** Set the can in the sink to thaw, then pour out the water and dry the can. Place a small candle inside and light it with a long match.

# Temporary Sculpture

**Materials Needed:**
- Building blocks
- Miscellaneous sculptural elements (see step 1)
- Modeling clay *or* play dough

**Type of Activity:** Design and sculpture
**Object:** Make a no-fuss, no-mess, temporary sculpture
**Ages:** 6 and older

**1** Along with building blocks, assemble an array of objects you don't normally think of as being compatible with blocks: wheels, orbs, Legos, small toys, shells, twigs, and so on.

**2** Using clay to stick various objects together, you can stack things in a way that gravity won't normally allow . . .

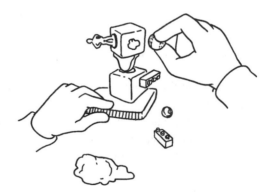

**3** . . . or create a unique collage-type sculpture. It's easy to change if you try things and don't like them. Have fun!

# Wire Sculpture

**Type of Activity:** Sculpture
**Object:** Use common wire to make shapes of all kinds
**Ages:** 8 and older

**Materials Needed:**
• Paper
• A pencil
• Thin wire
• Wire cutters *or* old scissors that can cut your wire
• Pliers
• A small wooden slab for the base
• Nails (some without heads for Variation)
• A hammer

**1** Decide on the shape you want to fashion from wire, and draw it on paper.

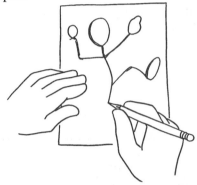

**2** Choose any thin wire that bends easily, either plastic covered or plain. Don't choose wire so thin that it can cut your fingers as you handle it. To start, cut off about 6 feet and find the midpoint.

**3** Usually, it works out well to place the midpoint of your wire at the topmost point of the shape. Start shaping the wire down from that point, shaping one side and then the other. Use pliers for crimping sharp angles.

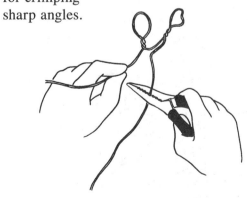

**4** If you run short of wire, add more length by twist-knotting extra feet onto the end. Pliers come in handy for this.

**5** Shape a base with the last few inches of both ends of the wire. Nail this to the wood.

**Hint:** This wire sculpture looks a lot like a line drawing, and looks best silhouetted against a plain background.

## Variation:

**1** Draw a simple shape, such as a butterfly, on paper. Lay it on the board.

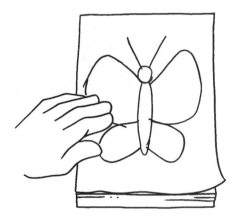

**2** At every point where the outline of the butterfly changes direction, hammer in a headless nail.

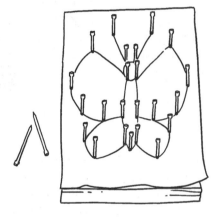

**3** Twist the wire from nail to nail, forming the shape of the drawing.

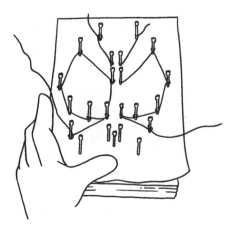

**4** Lift the shape off of the nails—voilà!

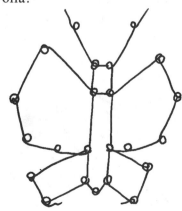

# Straw Sculpture

**Materials Needed:**
• Paper straws
• Scissors
• Glue
• A block of wood for the base (optional)

**Type of Activity:** Assembly sculpture
**Object:** Use common drinking straws to shape a quick modular sculpture
**Ages:** 6 and older

**1** Think of something real to sculpt that has lots of straight lines in it—a log cabin, a jungle gym. Or designing an abstract shape is great, too. Either way, it helps to start out with a plan!

**2** Cut straws into many lengths to give you a variety of building shapes.

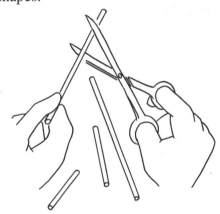

**3** There are several ways to connect straws together. You can shove them inside each other at the ends (an angle cut may help), using glue or not (A); you can simply glue them together, at any angle (B); you can glue them together parallel (C); or you can notch them slightly and fit them together so that the intersection lies flat (D). You can connect them any way you can think of!

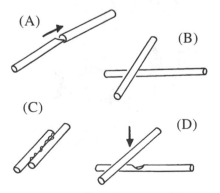

(A)

(B)

(C)

(D)

**4** When your construction is complete, glue it to a board if you like.

# Mobile Mania

**Materials Needed:**
See individual mobiles, and substitute freely with whatever you have around the house, garage, or yard.

**Type of Activity:** Assembly and construction
**Object:** Use almost anything you can think of to create a hanging sculpture
**Ages:** 6 and older

## #1 Aqua Mobile

**Materials Needed:**
- Construction paper
- A pencil
- Scissors
- Colored markers
- Light string, dental floss, *or* fishing line
- An 18-inch (or so) piece of slim bamboo

**1** Draw and cut out aqua creatures—fish, sea horses, starfish, and so on. Color both sides, then make small holes in the tops with the point of the scissors.

**2** String them up to your length of bamboo. Use different lengths of string.

**3** Cut a string about half-again as long as the bamboo. Attach it to both ends of the bamboo as a suspension string. Hang your mobile where a breeze can get to it.

# #2 Seashell Mobile

**Materials Needed:**
- Your favorite shell finds from the beach
- Light string, dental floss, *or* fishing line
- Superglue
- A stick of driftwood

**1** Some shells have been naturally pierced by predators or by the abrasion of the waves. For the ones that aren't, fashion string loops and glue them to the shells.

**2** Thread the shells with string, and attach the string to the driftwood so that they hang interestingly at different lengths and angles.

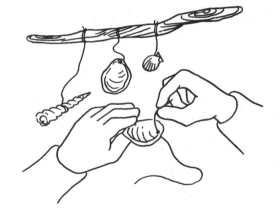

**3** Cut a string about half-again as long as the stick of driftwood. Attach it to both ends of the wood as a suspension string. Hang your mobile where it will remind you of your trip to the shore.

# #3 Celestial Mobile

**Materials Needed:**
- Construction paper
- A pencil
- Scissors
- Colored cellophane
- Glue
- A bendable wire clothes hanger
- Pliers
- Light string, dental floss, *or* fishing line

**1** Draw a sun shape and seven smaller star, moon, and sun shapes. Cut them all out.

**2** Cut out their centers so each figure becomes just a thick border. Trace and cut out an exact copy of each one, for a total of eight sets of identically shaped borders.

**3** Sandwich and glue a piece of colored cellophane inside each set. Trim away the excess cellophane.

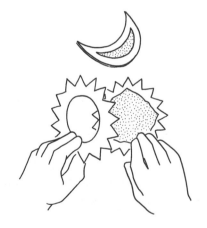

**4** Pierce the top corner of each figure.

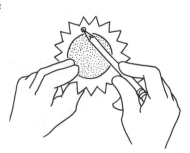

**5** Shape the clothes hanger into a circle. Use pliers if it helps.

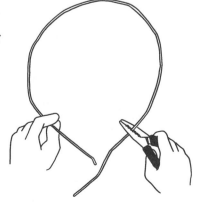

**6** String the cellophane celestial bodies within the circle. To keep them well placed, you can fasten each from top and bottom, and use a little tape or glue to keep them from sliding. Hang the circled wire from a string in a place where the sun will shine through!

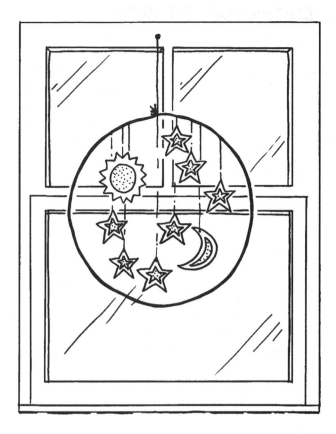

# III. Nature's Way

## Plants, Leaves, Seeds, and Fruits

# Air-Drying Flowers and Plants

**Materials Needed:**
- Fresh flowers, other plants (see Hint)
- Rubber bands
- String
- Scissors
- Amber cellophane (optional)

**Type of Activity:** Handling and preserving botanicals

**Object:** Preserve spring plants for year-round beauty

**Ages:** 6 and older

**1** With rubber bands, tightly bind the flowers together in bunches of three or four.

**2** Cut a couple of feet of string and tie it to the rubber band of each bunch. Hang the bunches heads down, not touching any surface. A warm, dry, dark attic or closet is perfect.

**3** Sunlight will fade brightly colored blossoms. If you have no place to hang them away from the light, cover each bundle with a generous wrapping of amber cellophane. Keep the cellophane open at top and bottom.

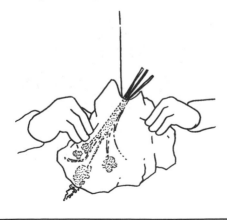

**4** When the flowers are completely dry (probably a week or more, depending on the flower), arrange them in an attractive vase.

**Hint:** Many, many flowers can be air-dried. Queen Anne's lace, goldenrod, clover, hydrangea, baby's breath, heather, and lavender are just a few. Also good are grasses, oats, and wheat, as well as marsh rushes, milkweed pods, yucca pods, and pussy willows. Fleshier blossoms tend to decompose and dry better with the powder method (see the next activity, Powder-Drying Flowers and Plants).

## Variation:

Another air-drying method—if you have space—is simply to spread the plants in a single layer on tissue paper or newspaper, cover them with another sheet of paper, and leave them to dry.

# Powder-Drying Flowers and Plants

**Materials Needed:**
- Powdered borax
- Cornmeal (see Variation)
- A plastic *or* cardboard box with a tightly fitting lid, large enough for your chosen plants
- Fresh flowers and plants—virtually any will work

**Type of Activity:** Handling and preserving botanicals
**Object:** Preserve spring plants for year-round beauty
**Ages:** 8 and older

**1** Thoroughly mix one part borax with two parts cornmeal. Put a layer of this mixture (at least ½ inch) in the bottom of the box.

**2** Arrange the plants on top of the powder so that they do not touch. Cover them with another layer of the powder mixture.

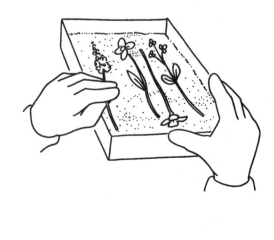

**3** Put the lid on the box and stash it in a dry place, at room temperature, for 3 to 4 weeks.

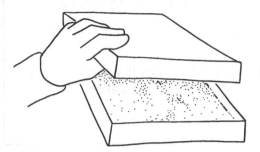

**4** When the plants have dried, gently remove them from the box, shake the powder off, and arrange them in an attractive vase.

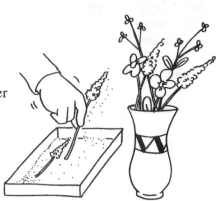

## Variation:

A powder mixture can also be made by mixing two parts borax with one part sand. Use the kind of sand sold for sandboxes—not salty beach sand. This powder dries the flowers faster, but check your plants often and remove them as soon as they're dry, or they could fade badly.

# Pressing Flowers and Plants

**Materials Needed:**
- Flowers and plants (see Hint)
- Sheets of newspaper, tissue paper, *or* plain paper towels
- Sheets of cardboard
- Weights, such as large heavy books, bricks, *or* concrete blocks

**Type of Activity:** Handling and preserving botanicals
**Object:** Save the plants of spring for year-round beauty
**Ages:** 8 and older

**1** Stack three sheets of paper, and arrange a few plants—just the way you want each to dry—on the top sheet.

**2** Cover the plants with a second layer of several sheets of paper.

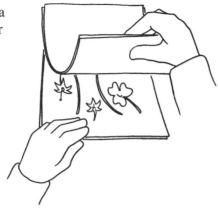

**3** Repeat with many layers of flowers and papers.

**4** Top the pile off with a sheet of cardboard. Cover the cardboard with weights, and keep the pages pressed for about 1 week for delicate flowers or several weeks for sturdier ones.

**5** Your pressed flowers are dry and flat—and somewhat delicate.

## Variation:
You can also create a plant press with two pieces of board and C-clamps. Arrange your plants between sheets of paper as described, then sandwich the pile between two boards and compress it with the C-clamps.

**Hint:** Many delicate flowers and plants dry best under pressure. Buttercups, larkspur, periwinkle, violets, columbine, and ferns are just a few. You can also press flowers as sturdy as roses or carnations, but they will take longer to dry. They can be framed under glass for wall art or under cellophane for greeting cards.

# Watch It Grow

**Materials Needed:**
- A potato *or* other vegetable or fruit (see step 1)
- A glass container (see step 1 and Variations)
- Water
- Toothpicks
- Seeds (such as you might buy in little packets for gardening) *or* dried beans (such as lima, kidney, or lentils) from your kitchen cabinet
- Paper towels (see Variations)
- A clean, new kitchen sponge (see Variations)

**Type of Activity:** Gardening indoors
**Object:** Grow plants so you can watch as they grow
**Ages:** 5 and older

---

**1** Choose a whole potato, beet, onion, or garlic; or the top of a carrot, pineapple, or turnip; or an avocado pit; or experiment with what you have at hand. Choose a vessel of clear glass—a goblet, jar, or vase—into which your vegetable or fruit will fit with just a little room to spare.

**2** Half fill your vessel with water. Pierce your vegetable or fruit with three or four toothpicks and suspend it in the vessel.

**3** Place it where it will get some sunlight, and watch it grow.

## Variation:
- Spread several paper towels on the bottom of a baking dish. Wet the towels thoroughly, and sprinkle seeds or beans on top. Keep them wet, and watch them sprout and grow.

- Curl a clean, dry kitchen sponge inside a jar or drinking glass. Wedge seeds in between the sponge and the inside of the glass. Dribble water into the top edge of the sponge until it's thoroughly moist. Keep the sponge wet, and watch those seeds grow.

# Shape-and-Grow Topiary

**Type of Activity:** Gardening sculpture
**Object:** Create an ivy star
**Ages:** 8 and older

**Materials Needed:**
- A 4- to 6-foot length of wire
- Pliers
- A clay pot
- Wire cutters
- Potting soil
- Two or three young ivy *or* other vines, with roots
- Water
- Twist ties

**1** Shape one end of the wire into a circular base. Size the circle so that it fits in the bottom of the pot.

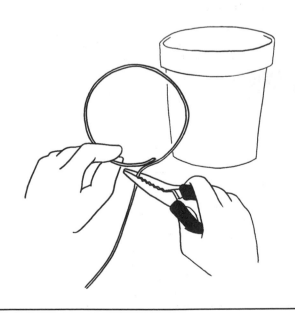

**2** Using the pliers, shape the other end of the wire into a star. Cross the wire through the middle of the star several times. If you still have extra wire, snip it off, or double it back to further strengthen the outline.

**3** Set the base in the pot. Fill the container with potting soil and plant the ivy sprouts. Water the soil thoroughly.

**4** Over the months, as the ivy grows up along the form, use twist ties to force it to twine where you want. You can remove these later.

**5** Six months later: Wow, an ivy star!

# Terrific Terrarium

**Type of Activity:** Gardening indoors
**Object:** Create a gardenscape in an aquarium or a large jar
**Ages:** 7 and older

**Materials Needed:**
• An oversize jar (1 to 10 gallons or more) *or* a fish aquarium, with a lid (see step 4)
• Plants (see step 1)
• Gravel (from a gardening store)
• Charcoal (from a pet or aquarium store)
• Potting soil
• Water
• Plastic wrap *or* clear plastic (optional, see step 4)

**1** Choose plants—ferns, mosses, African violets—that flourish in high humidity. Select sizes appropriate for your container.

**2** At the bottom of your container, layer first an inch of gravel, then about half that much charcoal, then at least 2 inches of potting soil.

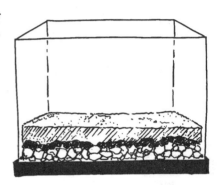

**3** Look at your plants and plan a balanced composition of color, texture, and height. One by one, make a shallow depression in the soil, put a plant's roots in, and pack soil around it gently.

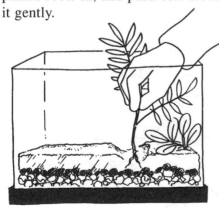

**4** Water the soil lightly, and sprinkle water on the leaves, too. Cover the container. If it didn't come with a lid, fashion one from clear plastic or plastic wrap. Water sparsely over time—there won't be much evaporation.

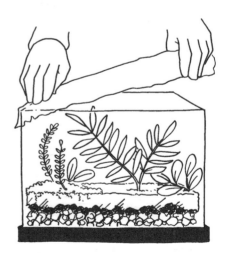

## Variation:

Make a cacti garden in a shallow dish. Use sandy soil and do not cover the arrangement.

# Autumn Dragon

**Type of Activity:** Leaf gathering, drawing, and gluing

**Object:** Create a collage dragon from autumn's bits and pieces

**Ages:** 6 and older

**Materials Needed:**
- Dry leaves and grasses
- A sheet of sturdy paper, lightweight cardboard, *or* poster board
- A pencil
- Colored markers
- Glue
- Scissors

**1** From your yard or the park, collect a supply of sturdy dried leaves and grasses, including pods and seeds if available. Choose generous amounts of each type.

**2** On paper (or cardboard), draw the basic outline for your dragon (or any other design you choose).

**3** Draw and color the eye and the fiery tongue.

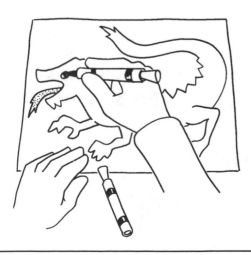

**4** Glue on leaves and other bits to create scales, wings, claws. Clip and trim to get the shapes you want.

**5** Continue until all drawn lines are covered and the dragon is filled in.

**Variation:**
Shape the word "Welcome," frame it, and hang it on the front porch.

# Beany Mosaic

**Type of Activity:** Drawing, bean choosing, and gluing
**Object:** Create a mosaic from seeds and beans
**Ages:** 7 and older

**Materials Needed:**
• A sheet of stiff cardboard *or* light (smooth-surfaced) wood
• A pencil
• Several types of beans and seeds (see step 2)
• Glue
• A brush

**1** Draw the outline of your mosaic on your cardboard.

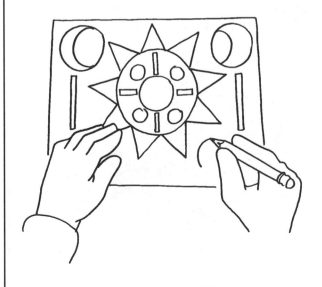

**2** For your mosaic chips, choose dried beans (lima, kidney) and peas (black-eyed, split green), seeds (pumpkin, sunflower), berries (holly, sumac), birdseed, peppercorns, and so on. Arrange them in separate piles or batches.

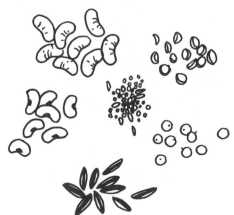

**3** Brush glue onto your picture, one section at a time. Fill each section with a single type (or combination) of chip. Cover the area completely.

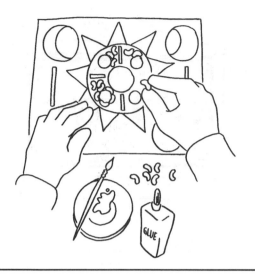

**4** Continue until you have completed the entire mosaic.

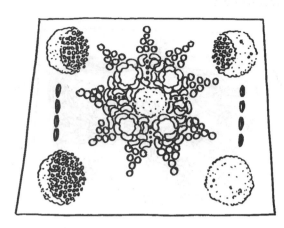

# Seedy Necklace

**Type of Activity:** Bead threading
**Object:** Create a cute necklace from seeds
**Ages:** 8 and older

**Materials Needed:**
• Clean, dried seeds (see step 1)
• A paintbrush
• Paints
• A scrap of wooden board
• A small, sharp nail
• A hammer
• A large needle
• Embroidery thread
• Varnish (optional)

**1** Pumpkin seeds are a good choice, as are any melon or gourd seeds. Assemble a generous amount, all of one kind or a variety.

**2** Decide what colors to make your necklace. Paint the seeds accordingly.

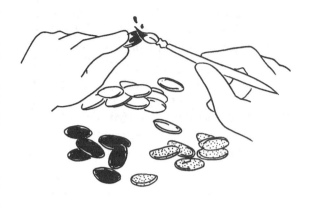

**3** When the paint is dry, place the seeds on the board. With the hammer and nail, pierce each seed in about the same place.

**4** With the needle and using embroidery thread of a complementary color, thread the seeds into a necklace. Make it large enough to slip over the head of the wearer, then tie it off.

## Variations:

Some seeds look so beautiful in their natural state that they need no paint; you might just use them as they are, or varnish them for shine and to keep their natural color.

# Peachy Ring Choker

**Type of Activity:** Rubbing and threading
**Object:** Create a cute necklace from peach pits
**Ages:** 9 and older

**Materials Needed:**
- 15 or more whole, large peach pits, clean and dry (see step 1)
- A sidewalk *or* other area with rough pavement
- A metal file
- Decorative cord *or* ribbon
- A necklace fastener (from a craft store)
- Paint *or* varnish and brushes (optional)

**1** Rub each peach pit hard on the rough pavement, first on one side, then on the other. The goal is to break through to the center. When the opening is large enough, push out the soft seed in the center and discard it (or save it for use in another project). The number of pits you'll need depends on their size and the length of necklace you want.

**2** If the tips of the pits are sharp, rub them smooth, and file off any other rough edges.

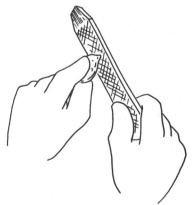

## Variations:

Peach rings have an interesting texture just as they are, but you can varnish them for shine or paint them to match your ribbons and cord.

**3** Thread the rings onto two strands of cord or ribbon, or ribbon and cord mixed, weaving the strands alternately in and out.

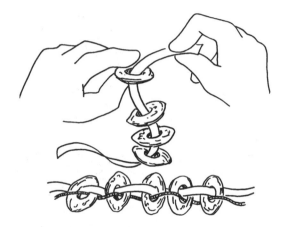

**4** For closure, tie each strand securely to the final rings at both ends, leaving enough extra to attach your store-bought clasp.

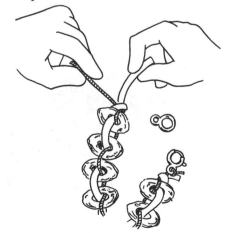

# Citrus Scenter

**Type of Activity:** Assembly
**Object:** Create a handsome scent ball
**Ages:** 7 and older

**Materials Needed:**
- A fresh lemon *or* orange
- A ribbon (18 inches or so) in a complementary color to the fruit
- Thumbtacks *or* straight pins (optional)
- Whole cloves

**1** Circle the lemon or orange with ribbon. Criss-cross the ribbon and circle the fruit again, then tie an attractive bow on the top.

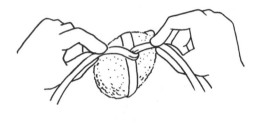

**2** If the ribbon is too slippery, secure it to the fruit with tacks at the crisscross and on top, or pierce the ribbon in several places with straight pins, or both.

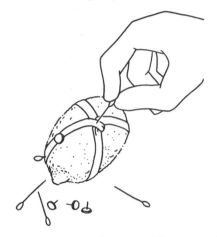

**3** Push whole cloves into the fruit, covering the entire surface.

**4** Scenters are attractive enough to be hung in full view. (You can also put them in drawers, closets, or cars, or use them as part of a holiday centerpiece.)

# Corn Husk Doll

**Materials Needed:**
- Dried corn husk leaves (see Hint)
- A pan of water
- One thick, full husk with the stem still attached
- Light string *or* embroidery thread *or* small rubber bands
- Colored-ball straight pins *or* pushpins
- Cloth and ribbon (optional, see step 8)

**Type of Activity:** Assembly
**Object:** Create a doll from the frontier days
**Ages:** 9 and older

**1** Smooth the husk leaves, and put a few in the water. These will be pliable for bending and knotting.

**2** Tie a wet husk around the center of the full husk for a waist.

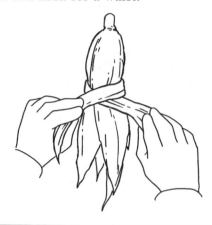

**3** For the head, crumple some dry husk scraps into a small ball. Fold one husk in half, place the crumpled ball inside it, and tie it at the neck with string or secure it with a rubber band.

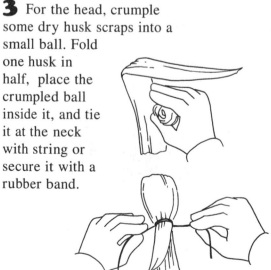

**4** Place the head over the stem of the full husk. Circle and tie it with a thin strip of wet husk to form a neck.

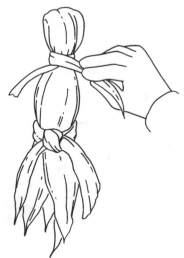

**5** For arms, roll two of the wet leaves over on their width, then fold each over and tie the pointed edges (the hands).

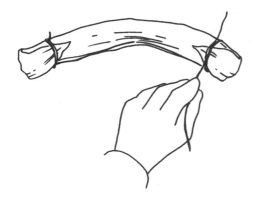

**6** Cross the ends of the arms over each other on the back of the body. Tie them firmly with a crisscross harness of string. Use pins for facial features. You have a pioneer girl in her long skirt.

**7** To transform the doll into a boy, separate the "skirt" in two and tie off each half at the bottom to form trouser legs.

**8** Use scraps of fabric, ribbon, construction paper, pipe cleaners, old jewelry, or whatever is at hand to dress and decorate your doll.

**Hint:** Dried corn husks come with the decorative Indian corn sold in the autumn. In the summer, green husks cover fresh corn on the cob. You can spread these out in a single layer on newspaper and leave them in a warm place to dry—one week to a month, depending on temperature and humidity.

# Go Peanuts!

**Type of Activity:** Assembling and painting
**Object:** Create playthings and decorative items from peanut shells
**Ages:** 7 and older

**Materials Needed:**
• Clean, dry, empty peanut shells, singles and doubles
• Scissors
• A pipe cleaner (long ones work best)
• Glue
• A clay pot filled with small, attractive stones
• Acrylic paints
• A paintbrush
• Jewelry rings (from the craft store)
• A large needle *or* small, sharp nail

## #1 Nut Buttercup

**1** Select five single-nut shell halves. Trim their edges down to make them more shallow.

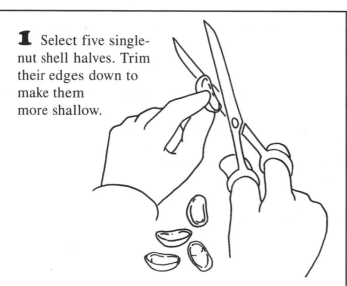

**2** Roll one end of the pipe cleaner into a small, closed circle.

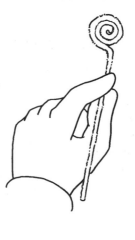

**3** Glue the petals around the pipe cleaner circle. It's OK if you can still see a bit of pipe cleaner in the middle of the petals.

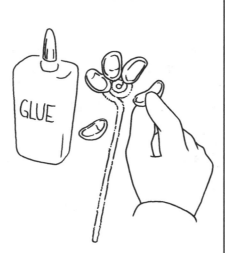

**4** Glue a small peanut shell tip or a chip in the center of the petals to hide the pipe cleaner.

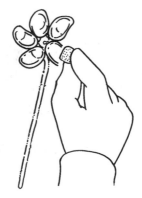

**5** Choose your largest double-nut shell halves and glue them to the pipe cleaner for leaves.

**6** Plant the buttercup in the pot of stones. Paint the petals yellow, the center chip white with black dots, and the leaves and stem green.

## #2 Ladybug Jewels

**1** Select a number of single-nut shell halves of similar size.

**2** With the needle or nail, pierce each one in the same place, near one end.

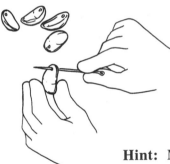

**Hint:** Make quick earrings by hanging two ladybugs onto plain pieced-ear wires (available at craft stores). Or, string one or more onto a simple chain for a necklace.

**3** Paint them black and red in the pattern of a ladybug. The black paint goes on the pierced part.

**4** Insert the jewelry rings in the holes you made in step 2.

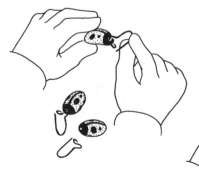

# Great Outdoors

# Bug Catcher

**Type of Activity:** Paper cut and glue
**Object:** To make a bug cage
**Ages:** 7 and older

**Materials Needed:**
• Tape measure
• Two empty, clean cans (the kind pineapple rings, tuna, or cat food come in), both the same size
• Scissors *or* cutters for wire screen
• Screen (metal or stiff plastic)
• Modeling clay (the kind that won't dry out)
• Wire, pipe cleaners, *or* sturdy tape

**1** Measure the circumference of one of your cans. Cut a rectangular piece of screen that measures the distance of the circumference on one side and 6 to 8 inches on the other side.

**2** Roll the screen into a tube. It should fit snugly into the can; seal the seam of the tube with twists of wire or pipe cleaner or sturdy (duct) tape.

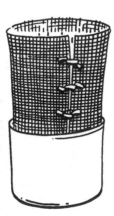

**3** Push the roll of screen down into the bottom of one of the cans; use the modeling clay to "weld" it into place.

**4** Go after your bug! When you catch it, use the second can for the lid.

# Backyard Birdhouse

**Type of Activity:** Light carpentry
**Object:** Build a home for your bird friends
**Ages:** 10 and older—*Adult Supervision*

**Materials Needed:**
- A board measuring 5 feet 6 inches by 6 inches by 1 inch (pine is easiest to saw)
- A pencil
- A ruler
- A saw
- Many small carpentry nails
- A hammer
- Four to six 3-inch nails
- A step ladder
- Paint and a brush (optional)

**1** With your pencil and ruler, measure and mark the board as shown in the diagram. Measure again to be safe.

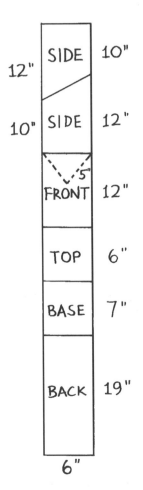

| | | |
|---|---|---|
| 12" | SIDE | 10" |
| 10" | SIDE | 12" |
| | FRONT 5" | 12" |
| | TOP | 6" |
| | BASE | 7" |
| | BACK | 19" |

6"

**2** Label the pieces and saw along the lines, including sawing a triangular opening (5 by 5 by 6 inches) in the front.

**3** Using the small nails, nail the sides to the back (1 inch from the bottom), the bottom to the sides, and the front onto this. The front should extend about 2 inches above the sides. The back also extends 5 inches above the birdhouse.

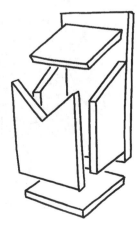

165

**4** Lay the top on the house. It should lie snug inside the inner edge of the front panel.

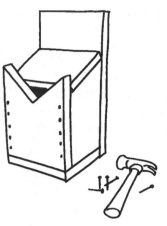

**5** Use 3-inch nails to secure the house to a tree. Paint it if you like.

**Note:** Cats in the neighborhood? Visit your local gardening shop or hardware store and buy a tree "cat cuff" before luring birds into cat territory.

# Pine-Butter Bird Feeder

**Type of Activity:** Assembly
**Object:** Build a feeder for your bird friends
**Ages:** 7 and older

**Materials Needed:**
• A large pine cone with the petals open
• Several feet of twine
• Peanut butter
• A spoon
• Birdseed

**1** Loop twine around several rows of petals on the small end of the pine cone.

**2** Push peanut butter in among the petals of the pine cone.

PEANUT

**3** Press birdseed into the peanut butter until the cone is covered.

**4** Hang the pine cone where the birds can get to it, and watch them gobble!

**Hint:** See the Note about cat cuffs in Backyard Birdhouse (page 166).

# Donut Bird Feeder

**Type of Activity:** Assembly
**Object:** Build a feeder for your bird friends
**Ages:** 8 and older

**Materials Needed:**
• Two jar lids *or* plastic lids
• A hammer
• A long (3- to 4-inch) nail
• A donut *or* bagel
• Pliers
• String

**1** Make a hole in the center of both lids using the hammer and nail.

**2** Set the nail on its head, and stack onto it one lid (rim up), the donut, then the second lid (rim down).

**3** Bend the point of the nail to make the "sandwich" snug.

**4** Tie the string around the nail head and hang the feeder outdoors. Birds love donuts as much as kids do.

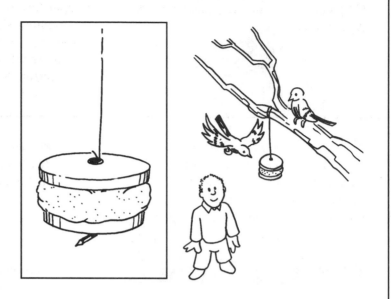

## Variation:

Buy a very long nut-and-bolt in a hardware store. With this, use the basic instructions here to fashion a feeder that holds several donuts and bagels.

**Hint:** See the Note about cat cuffs in Backyard Birdhouse (page 166).

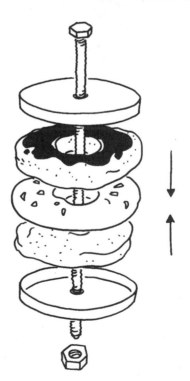

# Fish Print

**Type of Activity:** Printing
**Object:** Use a unique printing block
**Ages:** 8 and older

**Materials Needed:**
- A real, whole fish
- Water
- Bar soap
- Paper towels
- A medium-size paintbrush
- Nontoxic, water-soluble ink
- Large sheets of blank newsprint paper, shelf paper, *or* rice paper (See Hint)

**1** At the fish shop, choose the flattest fish you see—a small flounder is perfect. It should be whole (with fish and tail) and uncleaned (not scaled or gutted). Before beginning, wash the fish with mild soap, rinse it, and pat it dry with paper towels.

**2** Brush ink on one side of the fish. Brush with, not against the scales. Ink the head, fin, and tail thoroughly.

**3** Lay a sheet of paper over the inked fish and carefully press it down against every part of the surface.

**4** Lift the paper and see your print.

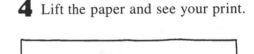

**Hint:** If your first try isn't perfect, experiment with different amounts of ink and different ways of applying and pressing the paper. It makes sense to practice on newspaper or cheap shelf paper. Save the expensive rice paper for when you've perfected your technique. Don't chance eating the fish—toss it when you're done.

# Shell Sculpting

**Type of Activity:** Designing and gluing
**Object:** Use the natural beauty of shells to make unique creations
**Ages:** 8 and older

**Materials Needed:**
- Shells (If you can find whole shells of the right size for these projects on the beach, great! Craft stores sell them too, as do gift shops in beach towns. Each project requires a certain type of shell.)
- Clear-drying glue
- Various other materials for individual projects

## #1 Shell Blossoms

**Additional Materials Needed:**
- Shells: for each blossom, four same-size halves of a bivalve (hinge-type) shell (cockles, mussels, *or* other) and a mini-shell for the center
- Dried wheat or grass (pick or make your own—see Air-Drying Flowers and Plants (page 144)
- A small (8 by 12 inches or so) rectangular wooden board, painted the color of your choice

**1** Arrange four shells like petals of a flower. Glue them together where they touch. Here they are shown with the hinge sides out, looking somewhat like dogwood blossoms.

**2** You can also arrange them with the hinges in, looking more like petunias.

**3** Putting the rounded side up also changes the way the blossoms look.

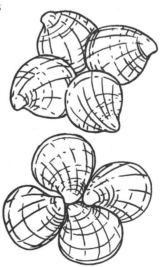

**4** Glue a tiny shell (such as a limpet) in the middle of each flower.

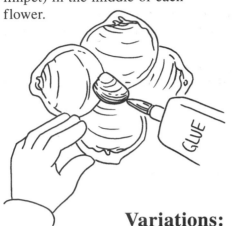

**5** Arrange oats, grasses, and shell blossoms into a still life against the board. Glue them all down.

## Variations:

In Chapter 2, Five Flower Stems (page 88) shows a number of ways to make stems. Most would work as well with shells as with paper flowers. You can make a bouquet of shell blossoms and arrange them in a vase with fresh greenery.

# #2 Shell Critters

**Additional Materials Needed:**
- Shells: choose them according to what you want to create, *or* make a creature that works well with what you have
- Toy eyes from the hobby store *or* black and white paint and a paintbrush
- Bits of string

**1 Mouse:** For the body use a lettered olive shell; for ears glue on limpets; the tail is a bit of string; the eyes are store-bought.

**2 Spider:** To a body of cowrie, glue legs made of jackknife clam shells, and then paint on some mean-looking eyes.

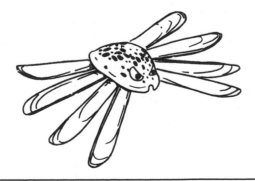

**3** **Tortoise:** How simple—a gorgeous speckled cowrie and four California cone legs, a periwinkle head, and an auger shell for a tail. No eyes needed!

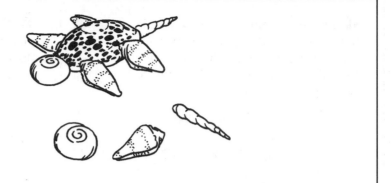

# #3 Shell Paper Weight

*Adult Supervision*

**Additional Materials Needed:**
- A medium-size wide-mouth jar with a leak-proof lid
- Shells: a variety of small and tiny ones
- Nonwater-soluble, clear-drying glue
- Extra-long tweezers (optional)
- A long, delicate brush
- A pile of beach rubble (finely crushed shells)
- Nonfloating glitter flakes
- A tablespoon
- Water
- Chlorine bleach

**1** Make sure the jar is perfectly clean. Select shells to use to create your seascape. It's a good idea to have one larger shell as a focal point.

**2** Glue the large shell inside the bottom of the jar as shown, then arrange the others around it. Long tweezers may help as the jar gets crowded. Allow the arrangement to dry completely.

**3** With the brush, dabble glue on the parts of the "sea bottom" that are still plain glass. Be careful not to get glue on the shells.

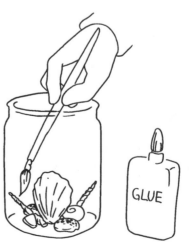

**4** Put in a handful of beach rubble. Screw on the lid, shake the jar gently, then set it down to let the glue dry. Repeat steps 3 and 4 until the bottom is completely covered.

**5** When the glue is completely dry, add a tablespoon or so of glitter flakes.

**6** Fill the jar to the brim with water plus 3 tablespoons of chlorine bleach, then screw the lid on securely.

**7** Shake—and see the phosphorescent sea foam.

# Shell Mobile

**Type of Activity:** Assembly
**Object:** Use the natural beauty of shells and driftwood to make a unique mobile
**Ages:** 8 and older

**Materials Needed:**
- Shells (see step 1)
- A sturdy, interesting-looking, large piece of driftwood for the brace
- Small screw eyes
- Clear-drying glue that will work with metal
- String *or* anything from thin, rough twine to gold thread
- Scissors

**1** You can buy fancy tropical shells, but it's more fun, if you can, to use what you find on a beach walk, from perfect scallops to scraps of whelk casing, from crab claws to small bits of driftwood.

**2** Put your large piece of driftwood (the brace) on the work surface. In front of it, arrange the mobile elements in a way that will look nice hanging.

**3** When your design is final, glue a screw eye onto the planned connecting points of each shell. You can screw them into the wood, rather than gluing, if it is sturdy enough. Make sure to include one on the top for hanging.

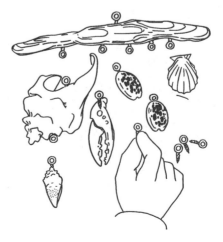

**4** Cut pieces of string, and tie the elements together.

**5** Hold the mobile up by the brace, and have a look at how it hangs. If you are not happy with how it looks at first, remove the string and reorganize or add elements.

# Driftwood Sculpture

**Type of Activity:** Assembly
**Object:** Use the natural beauty of driftwood to make an abstract sculpture
**Ages:** 8 and older

**Materials Needed:**
- Driftwood and other beach finds if desired (see step 1)
- A rectangular (*or* other shape) wooden board, painted if you like (see step 2)
- Small, headless nails
- A hammer
- Glue

**1** Collect a variety of sizes and types of driftwood. Add to the pile, if you like, shells, sea glass, and any other beach flotsam that catches your eye.

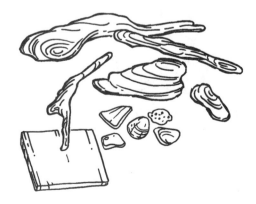

**2** As you begin to visualize your standing sculpture, choose a piece of wood that will support it as a base. Securely nail this "backbone" for your sculpture to the wooden board.

**3** Use your imagination and trial and error to add to your sculpture. You can make a complicated sculpture by gluing and nailing on all your favorite beach finds.

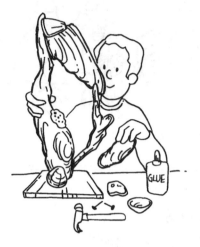

**4** However, some pieces of driftwood are so beautifully sculpted by nature that all you really need to do is display their best side.

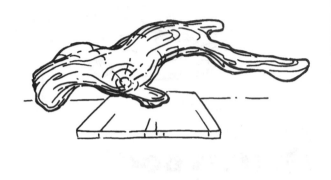

# Sand Painting

**Type of Activity:** Painting
**Object:** Use sand to create an original-looking painting
**Ages:** 8 and older

**Materials Needed:**
• A jar of sand
• Paper cups
• Dry tempera paint, colors of your choice
• Stiff cardboard *or* poster board
• A pencil
• A brush
• Clear glue
• Newspaper

**1** Put about ¼ cup of sand in a paper cup. Add one color of tempera powder, and stir well. The more tempera, the brighter the final color. Make a mixture in a cup for each color you want.

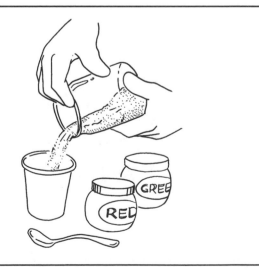

**2** Sketch the basics of your painting on the cardboard. Flowers are a good subject. You don't need a lot of detail; just make sure to outline the areas that will be different colors, such as petals, leaves, and the design of the vase.

**3** Paint glue thickly onto all the areas that will take one color—the green leaves, for instance. Pour the sand and green tempera mixture onto these areas. Then stand the board on its side and gently shake off the excess mixture onto a sheet of newspaper. Return the excess mixture to the green cup.

**4** Repeat with each section of the painting until the entire surface is colored, then set it aside to dry.

# Japanese Wind Sock

**Type of Activity:** Assembling and sewing
**Object:** Create a unique "kite"—the traditional Japanese carp wind sock
**Ages:** 9 and older

**Materials Needed:**
• A large plastic soda bottle
• A ruler *or* tape measure
• Scissors
• White fabric, 20 by 25 inches or larger
• An extra-soft pencil
• Newspaper
• Acrylic paints
• A paintbrush
• A needle and thread
• String

**1** Cut a 1- or 1½-inch-wide ring from the soda bottle. Measure the circumference of the ring.

**2** Fold the fabric in half lengthwise and draw the carp shape shown here, with the fabric folded-side down. Make the mouth (shown here on the left edge of the fabric near the ruler) slightly longer (about ¼ inch longer) than *one-half* the circumference of the plastic ring you just cut.

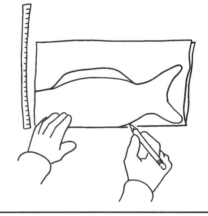

**3** Cut out the half-fish shape, making sure to cut through both layers, but leave the fold intact.

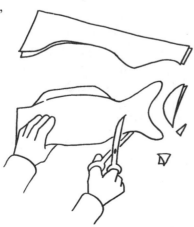

**4** Spread the cutout carp on newspaper. Paint it and allow it to dry.

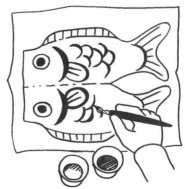

**5** Fold the carp inside out. Stitch it together by hand (or using a sewing machine) from the top of the mouth, along the fins, up to the end of the tail, leaving the mouth open and an opening in the tail (the wind must be able to blow through the fish).

**6** Turn the carp right-side out. Put the plastic ring in the mouth, then fold the fabric inward over the ring, and stitch it down. Also, tightly stitch the tail closed at the base of the tail fin.

**7** Cut a 2-foot length of string. Poke two small holes in both sides of the fish's mouth, and tie both ends of the string through the holes. Cut another length of string, 3 or 4 feet long, and attach this to the center of the first string.

**8** Attach the end of the long string to a pole or porch column, in a place where the wind can reach the carp and lift it up.

# Shadow Sundial

**Type of Activity:** Assembling and charting
**Object:** Build a sundial that works (on sunny days!)
**Ages:** 8 and older

**Materials Needed:**
- A tall, vertical flagpole *or* rod (see step 1)
- A sledgehammer *or* shovel (optional, see step 1)
- A clock *or* watch
- 12 large stones, smooth enough to write on with chalk
- Chalk
- Paint (optional)

**1** The easiest approach is to use a flagpole or fence post that stands out in the open. You could also drive (or dig a hole and insert) a pole of metal, wood, or PVC pipe into the ground into an open, unshaded area—with adult supervision, of course.

**2** One day, starting as soon as the sun comes up, go out to the pole every hour on the hour. At 6, 7, 8 o'clock and so on, put a stone down on the ground where the pole's shadow lies. Set each stone the same distance from the pole. They will begin to form a circle. Mark the hour on each stone with chalk as you set it down.

**3** In 12 hours, you will have placed stones in a semicircle; the unmarked half of the circle represents the dark, nighttime hours. The next day, use this sundial to tell time (roughly, anyway): when the shadow covers the 11 stone, it's 11 o'clock in the morning.

## Variation:
To make a more permanent sundial, paint the numbers on the stones.

**Hint:** As the seasons and the length of the days change, you will need to reset your sundial. Every 6 weeks or so (and at the beginning and end of daylight saving time), repeat step 2.

# Pinwheel

**Type of Activity:** Assembly
**Object:** Make a handmade pinwheel
**Ages:** 8 and older

**Materials Needed:**
• Paper of almost any kind *or* a sheet of plastic such as a transparency
• A pen
• A ruler
• Scissors
• Glue
• A brand-new pencil with an eraser
• A straight pin

**1** Cut out an 8- or 9-inch square of paper, and mark it into quarters as shown.

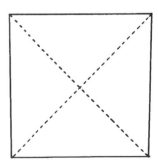

**2** Make cuts from each corner halfway to the center.

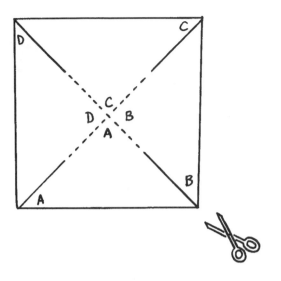

**3** Bend the four points (A, B, C, and D) in toward the center and glue them down to the corresponding A, B, C, and D spots shown here.

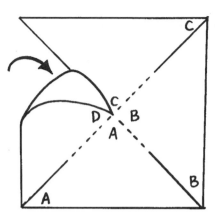

**4** With all four points glued down, you have the basic pinwheel shape. Stick the straight pin through the center.

**5** Push the straight pin through the pencil eraser. Leave it loose enough to spin. Blow and see it go. Loosen the pin if necessary.

# Plasti-Kite

**Type of Activity:** Assembly
**Object:** Make your own high-flying kite
**Ages:** 9 and older

**Materials Needed:**
• A rectangular plastic sheet approximately 30 by 48 inches (see step 1)
• Scissors
• A ruler
• A felt-tip pen and assorted permanent markers
• Two stiff, light dowels (wooden or plastic) 30 inches long (or the same length as the short side of the plastic sheet)
• Duct *or* other sturdy tape that sticks to plastic
• A spool of kite string

**1** You could use the kind of plastic sheeting that painters use for drop cloths, or even buy nylon. However, cutting open a large old plastic shopping bag or a plain old garbage bag works fine—and the lighter the plastic the better! When you've cut your sheet to the right size, fold it in half and mark off the lines with a felt-tip pen as shown.

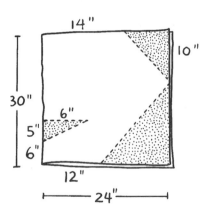

**2** Cut away the shaded areas. On a scrap of plastic, test to see that your markers won't smear when dry and that your tape adheres well.

**3** Unfold the sheet. Use the markers to brightly decorate your kite, coloring on both sides.

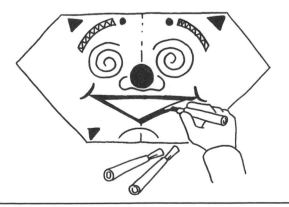

**4** Tape the dowels in place as shown, reinforce all corners and points with tape, and poke a very small hole through the tape at each wing tip.

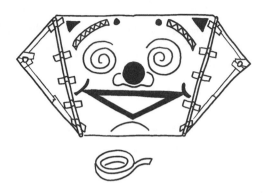

**6** Go fly your kite!

**5** Cut a 5- to 6-foot length of string and tie it from wing tip to wing tip. To this, tie the end of your spooled kite string.

# Pocket-Park Kite

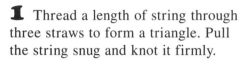

**Type of Activity:** Assembly
**Object:** Make a mini-kite for tight spaces
**Ages:** 9 and older

**Materials Needed:**
- Four 2-foot lengths of lightweight string (kite string, fishing line, dental floss)
- Six paper *or* plastic drinking straws
- Scissors
- Tissue paper *or* lightweight plastic from a trash bag
- A pencil
- Tape
- A spool of kite string

**1** Thread a length of string through three straws to form a triangle. Pull the string snug and knot it firmly.

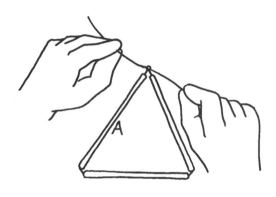

**2** String a second triangle of straws that shares side A with the first triangle.

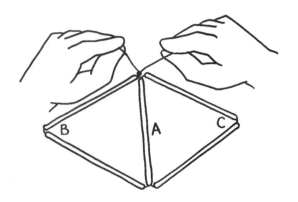

**3** Connect the two triangles with another straw-and-string at points B and C to form a pyramid.

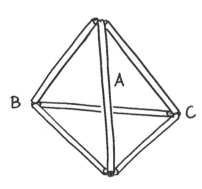

**4** Set the pyramid on tissue paper, trace a section that will cover two sides (with a generous hem), and cut it out.

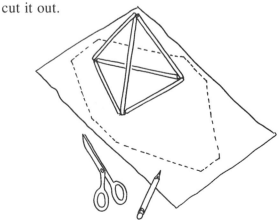

**5** Fold and tape the hem of the tissue over the straws to cover two sides and leave two open.

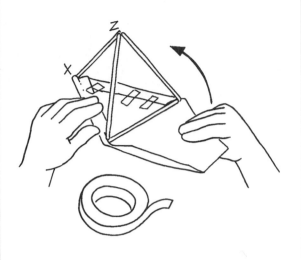

**6** Use scissors to pierce the straw that lies between the two covered sides at points X and Z. Insert the ends of a 2-foot length of string into these holes and knot them for the brace. Tie the end of your kite string to the middle of the brace string.

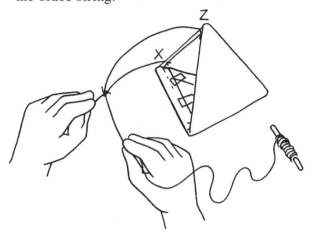

**7** Find some wind!

# Barometer

**Type of Activity:** Assembly
**Object:** Make a tool for measuring air pressure
**Ages:** 10 and older

**Materials Needed:**
- Scissors
- A balloon
- A clean dry glass *or* jar, clear and with no label
- Rubber bands
- A plastic drinking straw
- First aid *or* duct tape
- A sheet of lightweight cardboard, about 8 by 12 inches
- A pen *or* pencil

**1** Cut open the balloon and stretch it tautly over the glass, securing it tightly with rubber bands.

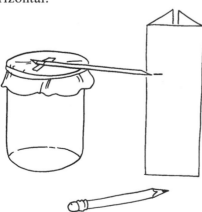

**2** Snip the ends of the straw to points and tape one end of the straw to the center of the stretched balloon. It should extend out horizontally.

**3** Fold the sheet of cardboard into thirds, lengthwise, and stand it on its end next to the glass. Mark a line for where the straw is when it's perfectly horizontal.

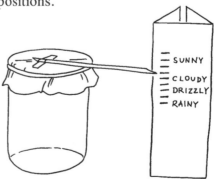

**4** Put the glass in a quiet, temperature-stable corner—not by a window or heat vent. As the weather changes in the next weeks, the straw should rise on sunny days, fall with rain. Mark and note the weather (cloudy, drizzly, and so on) at the straw's various positions.

SUNNY
CLOUDY
DRIZZLY
RAINY

**5** Once the chart is well noted, you should be able to check it and know the weather before you even look out the window.

# Sun Shades

**Type of Activity:** Assembly
**Object:** Keep the sun out of your eyes
**Ages:** 9 and older—*Adult Supervision*

**Materials Needed:**
• A 5-by-6-inch sheet of thick, corrugated cardboard
• A pencil
• A ruler
• A sharp knife
• White glue
• 15 or so inches of narrow, flat elastic

**1** Draw 11 lines, ½ inch apart, along the width of the piece of cardboard.

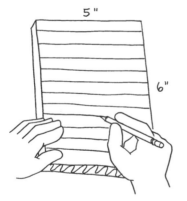

5 "

6 "

**2** Cut along each line. You should end up with 12 ½-inch-wide strips, each 5 inches long.

**3** Stack and glue the strips so that the corrugation is exposed. Then cut a nose hole.

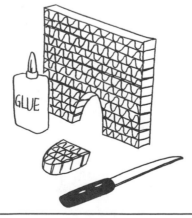

GLUE

**4** Attach both ends of the elastic band through the corrugation. Test the length—it should fit snugly around your head and rest on the bridge of your nose—before making the final knots.

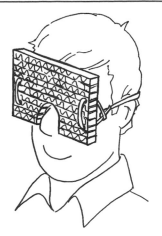

**Hint:** Wear these out on a bright, sunny day. You can see fine, and your eyes are shaded so that the sun doesn't bother them.

# Crystal Garden

**Type of Activity:** Simple chemistry
**Object:** Create an inorganic "garden"
**Ages:** 7 and older—*Adult Supervision*

**Materials Needed:**
- A handful of small stones
- A shallow bowl
- A coffee cup *or* small glass
- 1 tablespoon of ammonia
- 6 tablespoons each of: water, salt, and laundry bluing
- Food coloring

**1** Heap the stones in the bowl; in the cup, mix the ammonia, water, salt, and bluing.

**2** Pour the liquid over the stones, sprinkle in a few drops of food coloring, and set the bowl in a quiet corner.

**3** Check back in a couple of hours. The crystals will have begun to grow.

**4** Over several days, the crystals will grow more and more.

# Paperweights and Stone Pets

**Type of Activity:** Painting
**Object:** Turn ordinary stones into special mementos
**Ages:** 5 and older

**Materials Needed:**
• Smooth stones in many shapes and sizes
• A soft lead pencil
• Poster paints
• Paintbrush
• Varnish (optional)
• Glue

## #1 Decorated Stones

**1** Before starting to decorate, make sure the stones you select are perfectly clean and dry.

**2** Next, outline your drawing in pencil.

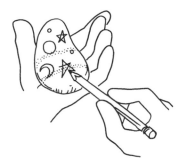

**3** Paint celestial bodies (moons and stars), flowers, whatever you like.

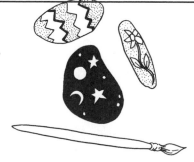

**Hint:** A paperweight makes a great Mother's or Father's Day gift. Coat stones with varnish after the paint has dried to keep the colors bright.

# #2  Pet Rocks

**1** Make sure the stones are perfectly clean and dry. Before starting to assemble, look at your stones. Do any seem to lend themselves to any particular creature?

**2** A tortoise, perhaps? Choose the right shape for the head, tail, and legs for a tortoise and glue them on.

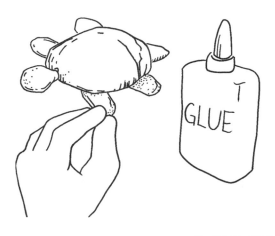

**3** Or make a snowman.

**4** Paint and varnish if you like. These make great, one-of-a-kind gifts.

# IV. In the Kitchen

## Cook—but Don't Eat It!

# Candle Creations

**Type of Activity:** Candle making
**Object:** Design and make your own candles
**Ages:** 7 and older—*Adult Supervision*

## #1  Dip Candle

**Materials Needed:**
- Wax (squares of plain wax are sold in craft stores, hardware stores, and some grocery stores), chopped in the needed amount
- A cutting board
- A knife
- A measuring cup
- At least four 1-pound coffee cans
- A large saucepan of water
- Various colors of crayons with paper removed
- Heat mittens
- Cotton twine
- Scissors
- Tongs
- Newspaper

**Additional Materials Needed:**
- A clothespin
- A clothes hanger

**1** You need a lot of wax for this project. Chop 8 cups or more. Put the chopped wax in a coffee can and put the can in the saucepan of water on the stove. Heat the wax until it is melted. To add color, break crayons in bits and stir until melted.

**2** When the wax is completely liquid, turn off the heat. Put on heat mitts, and move the pan with the can and hot water to your work surface. (Be sure to place it on a cutting board or a pad to protect the surface.)

**3** Cut a length of twine 6 inches longer than the depth of the can. Dip the twine into the wax and pull it straight out. Count slowly to 10 and dip again, again, and again, pausing each time to let the wax dry. It will take more than 100 dips to form a nice thick candle, tapered at both ends.

**4** When the candle is thick enough, use a clothespin to clip it to a clothes hanger to cool.

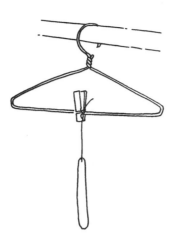

**5** You may carve one end so that your single candle will fit a candle holder.

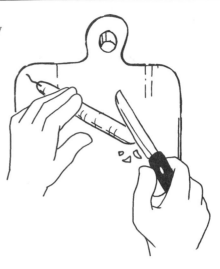

**6** Or, saw the candle slowly in half to result in two candles, carving the end of the bottom piece to expose the wick.

## #2 Multicolored Cup Candle

**Additional Materials Needed:**
• A small paper cup
• A coffee cup half filled with dried beans, stones, *or* sand

**1** Put about half a cup of chopped wax in each of three coffee cans. Add a crayon of a different color to each of the cans.

**2** Put one can of wax in the saucepan of water to melt. When the wax is liquid, put on heat mitts, remove the can from the water, and place the second can in the water.

**3** Cut a piece of twine long enough to circle the bottom of the paper cup and reach up past the rim (A). Use tongs to dip the twine in liquid wax (B).

(A)

(B)

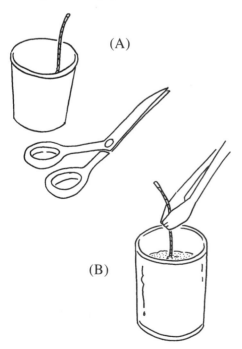

**4** Lay the twine on newspaper to dry for 5 minutes. Barely cover the bottom of the paper cup with one color of wax. Stick the twine wick you made down into the wax so that it rises from the center.

**5** When the wick has dried in place, pour ½ inch of the first color of wax into the cup. Rest the cup at an angle in the mouth of the coffee mug. Hold the wick in place in the center until it sets a bit.

**6** When the first wax poured into the cup is solid, pour in an inch or so of the second color. Rest the cup in the mug again, tilted in the opposite direction this time. Hold the wick in place in the center. Meanwhile, put the can with the third color of wax in the pan to melt.

**7** Repeat layering and angling with the three colors (remelting if necessary) until the cup is filled with alternating angles of wax. Finish with a level layer. When the candle is cooled and solid, trim the wick and peel off the paper cup.

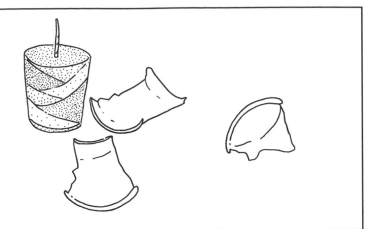

# #3 Crinkle Candle

**Additional Materials Needed:**
• Two small paper cups
• Chipped ice

**1** Use a coffee can and the saucepan to melt a cup of chopped wax. Add a crayon and allow to melt, for color.

**2** Cut a length of twine long enough to circle the bottom of a paper cup and reach up past the rim. Use tongs to dip the twine into the liquid wax. Lay the twine on the newspaper to dry for at least 5 minutes.

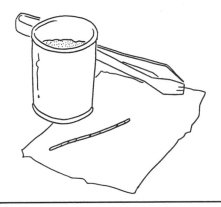

**3** Barely cover the bottom of the paper cup with wax. Stick the wick you made down into the wax so that it rises from the center. Allow it to cool.

**4** Fill the cup with chipped ice, keeping the wick in the center.

**5** Using mitts, pour the liquid wax into the cup.

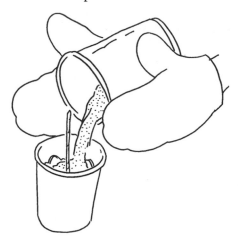

**6** When the wax is cool, hold the cup over the sink and peel off the paper. The melted ice will pour out.

**7** Voilà, a crinkly candle.

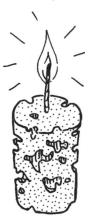

# #4 Sand Candle

**Additional Materials Needed:**
- A large bowl filled with clean, slightly damp sand
- A stick *or* stiff wire that will stretch across the mouth of the bowl

**1** Put 2 cups of chopped wax in a coffee can and melt it in the pan of water. Add a crayon for color.

**2** Cut a length of twine six inches longer than the depth of the bowl. With tongs, dip the twine into the liquid wax, leaving a few inches unwaxed. Lay the twine on newspaper to dry for 5 minutes.

**3** Make a deep, cup-shaped depression in the bowl of sand. A curvy shape is OK. Leave at least ½ inch of sand on the bottom of the bowl.

**4** Tie the unwaxed end of twine to the middle of the stick. Lay the stick over the mouth of the bowl so that the twine hangs down into the depression. Push this wick through the bottom layer of sand so it contacts the bowl and bends a little. Press a little sand back down around it.

**5** Slowly pour the liquid wax into the depression, filling it.

**6** When the wax is cooled and solid (20 minutes or more), lift the chunky candle up out of the sand.

**7** Flip it over so the sand side is up. Pick the wick up, and it's ready to light.

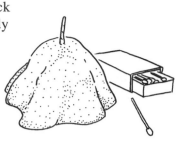

# Soap Crayons

**Type of Activity:** Mixing
**Object:** Create washable markers for bath toys
**Ages:** 5 and older

**Materials Needed:**
- 4½ cups of gentle, baby-safe soap flakes (e.g., Ivory)
- Water
- A measuring cup
- A mixing bowl
- A stirring spoon
- Three smaller plastic bowls
- Red, blue, and green food coloring
- A simple plastic sectioned ice tray

**1** Put the soap flakes and ¼ cup of water in the mixing bowl. Mix and mix and mix until you have a thick paste with no lumps.

**2** Separate the paste into three smaller bowls. To each, add 10 to 15 drops of a different color of food coloring. Mix each thoroughly.

**3** Press the paste into the sections of the ice cube tray. Set the tray in a warm, dry place for a couple of days until the paste is completely hardened.

**4** Pop out the cubes!

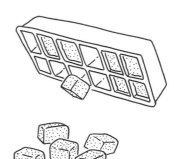

**Hint:** As tub toys, these are fun for writing on the tub and tile, and they wash off easily!

# Salty Dough Bread Basket

**Type of Activity:** Mixing and baking
**Object:** Create a special dough and sculpt with it
**Ages:** 9 and older—*Adult Supervision*

**Materials Needed:**
- 1½ cups of warm water
- 1¼ cups of salt
- A mixing bowl
- A stirring spoon
- 3½ cups of flour
- Cooking oil
- A rolling pin
- A ruler
- A knife
- An oval *or* rectangular glass *or* ceramic baking dish
- Spray varnish

**1** Put the water and salt in the mixing bowl. Mix until the salt is dissolved. Add 3½ cups of flour. Stir the mixture until it is smooth.

**2** Pull the mixture out of the bowl and put it on the table. Work the dough with your hands until it is smooth and elastic. Oil your fingers if they get sticky.

**3** Roll the dough into a ball. Oil it all over, and oil the rolling pin, too.

**4** Use the rolling pin to roll the dough out until it's about ¼ inch thick.

**5** Slice the dough into strips ¼ inch wide. Turn the baking dish upside down and lay five or six strips across the dish's bottom. Then start laying strips across the first strips in the opposite direction.

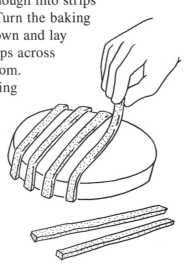

**6** Weave them by lifting and lowering the first strips.

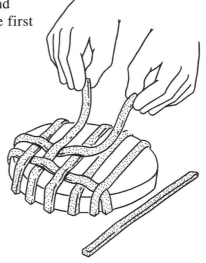

**7** If a strip runs short, "splice" it with another strip by wetting both ends slightly and pressing them gently together.

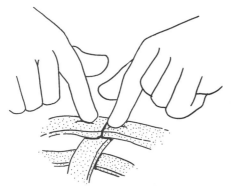

**8** Roll out a rope of dough with your hands.

**9** Moisten the rope and arrange it around the lip of the baking dish, attaching it (by pressing firmly but gently) to all the ends of the woven strips.

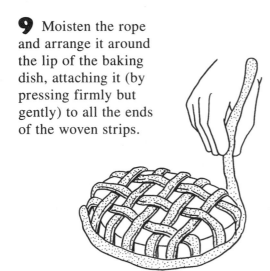

**10** Bake the dough at 325°F for an hour. When the baked dough is cool, lift it off the pan. Spray your basket with varnish in a well-ventilated place and allow it to dry.

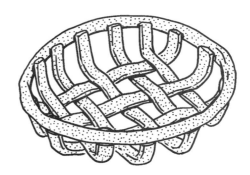

## Variations:

• Salt dough can be formed into many, many shapes, simple and complicated. For instance, you could shape uncooked dough into a snake. Before baking, etch a pattern on the skin with a knife. Use raisins or currants for eyes.

• Or, shape the dough into fruits and vegetables, and then paint them. You could even place these in the varnished bread basket.

# Pasta Mobile

**Type of Activity:** Assembly
**Object:** Create an all-pasta mobile
**Ages:** 8 and older—*Adult Supervision*

**Materials Needed:**
• Dried pasta of many shapes (see step 1 and Hint)
• ½ pound of round (not flat) spaghetti
• A large pot of boiling water
• A pencil
• Heat mitts
• Pliers
• A long pointed iron nail
• A non-Teflon cookie sheet
• A colander
• Cold water
• A 2-foot piece of string

**1** Gather spaghetti and several kinds of pastas—ones with holes (ziti, elbows) and ones without that can be pierced (lasagna). Put the spaghetti *only* in the boiling water and cook it according to directions on the package.

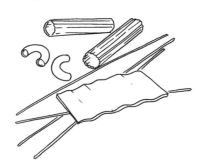

**2** Make a plan in your head for how to connect the dry pasta and cooked spaghetti. A piece or two of flat lasagna makes a good top brace. With a pencil, mark the spots on each piece where you'll pierce it. Include places to make holes for attaching the top string.

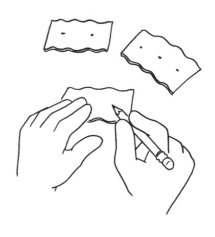

**3** Put the lasagna pieces on the cookie sheet. Turn on a burner on the stove, and put on heat mitts. Use the pliers to firmly grasp the nail, and hold the nail over the flame (or ring).

**4** When the nail is red hot, press the tip to the lasagna and the nail will burn right through.

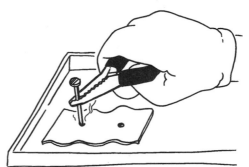

**5** Test the spaghetti for doneness. Drain it when it's al dente (a little stiff in the middle). Rinse it in cold water until it's no longer warm.

**6** Using your cooked spaghetti as the tie that binds, string up the dry pieces. Connect them by pushing the spaghetti through the pasta holes and knotting it.

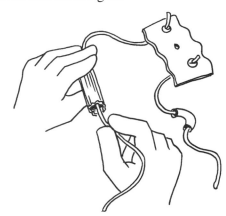

**7** Attach string to the top piece of pasta, and hang your mobile.

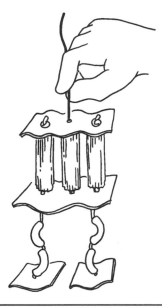

**Hint:** At stores where pasta is sold in bulk bins, you can buy just a few pieces of many kinds. If you find you have to buy many bags or boxes, make sure to seal up what you don't use and save it for cooking later.

# Volcano on the Counter

**Type of Activity:** Assembly
**Object:** Create a real erupting volcano
**Ages:** 10 and older

**Materials Needed:**
- A small empty can (such as for tuna or pineapple)
- A plastic cup large enough to overlap the empty can, with the bottom of the cup cut out
- Duct *or* masking tape
- A clay flowerpot with a hole in its bottom
- A baking dish large enough to hold the upside-down flowerpot
- Tinfoil
- Soup spoons
- Baking soda
- Dishwashing powder
- Red food coloring
- ½ cup of vinegar

**1** Tape the inverted cup to the open end of the can. Then seal them together with tape. Stack this on the bottom of the clay pot, and place the whole thing in the baking dish.

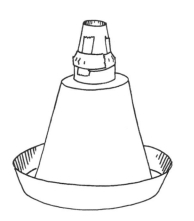

**2** Cover the form with crinkled tinfoil. Press the foil down through the open bottom of the plastic cup.

**3** Pour a soup spoon each of baking soda, dishwashing powder, and food coloring through the top hole. Finally, pour in the vinegar.

**4** Out it pours, like lava!

# Eggbird Mobile

**Type of Activity:** Assembly
**Object:** Make a light, fun mobile from empty eggshells
**Ages:** 8 and older

## Materials Needed:

- Six (or more) raw eggs
- A very long needle (¼ inch longer than an egg)
- Bowls
- Dishwashing detergent and water
- Construction paper
- Scissors
- Clear-drying glue
- Colored markers *or* paints and brushes
- Embroidery thread (see Hint)
- A leafless tree branch with many forks and twigs

**1** Empty each egg like this: With the needle, prick a small hole in the small end of the egg and a larger hole in the larger end (A). Holding the egg over a bowl, gently blow into the small hole (B). The egg comes slowly out the large end until the shell is empty. (Refrigerate the eggs in a covered container for other use.)

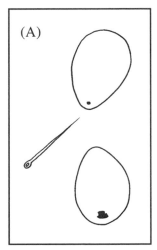 (A)

 (B)

**2** Very carefully wash and rinse the egg shells, then set them, large hole down, on a towel to dry.

**3** Cut triangular wings and tails from construction paper. Gently glue them to the shells.

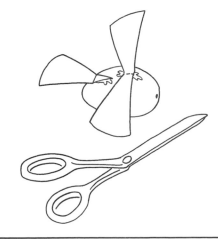

**4** Complete your bird decorations by drawing or painting eyes and beaks on each shell.

**5** Cut the thread into various lengths—10, 12, 14 inches, and so on— one for each shell. Use your long needle to run a length of embroidery thread through each shell.

**6** Hang the branch from a length of thread, then hang your birds from the sturdier twigs on your branch.

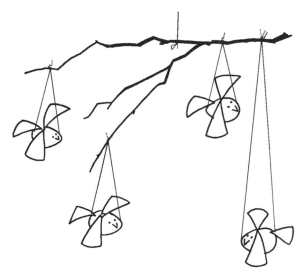

**Hint:** Choose your markers and threads in colors that match or look good together.

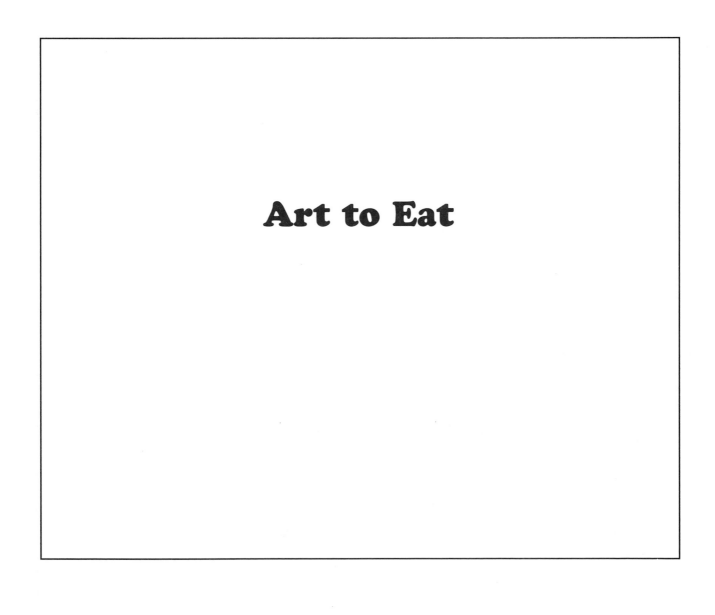

# Art to Eat

# Edible Neckwear

**Type of Activity:** Stringing
**Object:** Make edible party favors
**Ages:** 6 and older

**Materials Needed:**
• Dental floss *or* fishing line
• Scissors
• Life Savers and other hard candies with a hole in the center
• Fruit Loops *or* other brightly colored cereal with a hole in the center (or easily pierced)
• Extra-long shoestring licorice, red or black

## #1 Necklace for Her

**1** Cut a length of floss or fishing line that will make a nice long necklace for you (or a friend).

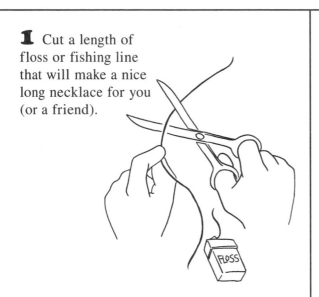

**2** String your edibles onto this line. You can do all candies, all cereals, or mix them up.

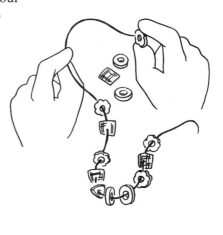

**3** When you have enough to fill the necklace, knot it and put it on. Mmmm—snacks to go.

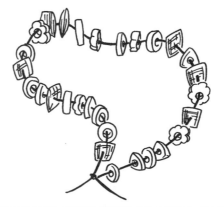

# #2 Boy's Bolo Tie

**1** Cut a 30-inch length of licorice, and drape it around the neck of the wearer.

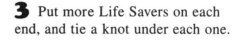

**2** Thread both ends through a single Life Saver. Knot each just below the candy to keep it from slipping.

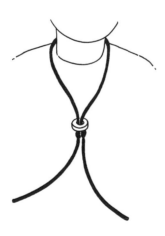

**3** Put more Life Savers on each end, and tie a knot under each one.

# Red Radish Roses

**Type of Activity:** Vegetable carving
**Object:** Make a beautiful vegetable center-
piece
**Ages:** 10 and older—*Adult Supervision*

**Materials Needed:**
• 12 radishes, clean, with the root ends sliced off
• A paring knife
• A bowl
• Ice water
• Thin bamboo skewers *or* 8- to 10-inch lengths of stiff wire
• 12 to 15 scallions
• Clean sand *or* gravel
• Parsley (optional)

**1** Peel the skin of each radish down in several strips, without detaching it. Put the radishes in a bowl of ice water in the fridge overnight.

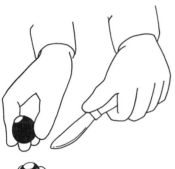

**2** Cut the bulb off each scallion. Then push a skewer or length of wire through each hollow stem.

**3** Attach a radish to the tip of the skewer where it emerges from the scallion stem.

**4** Fill the bowl almost to the brim with sand (or gravel). Push in the skewered scallion stems.

**Hint:** Sprinkle parsley on the surface of the sand for added natural effect.

# Blooming Carrots

**Materials Needed:**
- Cleaned, peeled carrots
- A paring knife
- A cutting board
- A bowl of cold water
- Toothpicks
- Cranberries *or* raisins

**Type of Activity:** Vegetable carving
**Object:** Make blooms from carrots
**Ages:** 10 and older—*Adult Supervision*

---

**1** Slice the carrots into very thin disks.

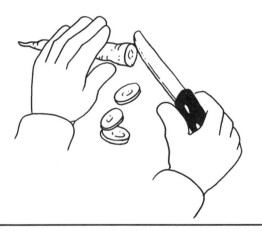

**2** Put all the disks in the bowl of water and store it in the fridge overnight. They will be twisted and curled by morning.

**3** Spear five or more carrot slices onto a toothpick, and top it with a cranberry or raisin.

**Hint:** Fashion the same scallion skewers as for Red Radish Roses (see facing page), then slip the toothpick part of the carrot blossom into the top of the scallion stem. A great addition to the radish centerpiece.

# Lemon Lilies

**Materials Needed:**
- Several pretty lemons
- A paring knife
- A shallow bowl filled with a layer of ice
- Dark, flat green leaves from any common shrubbery, rinsed

**Type of Activity:** Carving
**Object:** Create a refreshing centerpiece
**Ages:** 10 and older—*Adult Supervision*

**1** Carefully cut the lemons in half using a zigzag cut. Cut some lengthwise, some widthwise. Go all the way around, and cut deeply.

**2** Pull the halves apart.

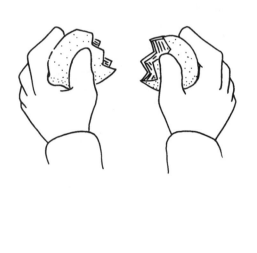

**3** Arrange the lemons on the ice. Arrange dark leaves around them.

**Hint:** Add a couple of Radish Roses or Blooming Carrots (without scallion skewers) from the two preceding activities.

# Marzipan Flowers

**Materials Needed:**
- Plain (uncolored) premade marzipan (see Hint)
- Toothpicks
- Food coloring
- A brush

**Type of Activity:** Sculpting
**Object:** Create cute candy blossoms
**Ages:** 6 and older

**1** Wash your hands! Pinch off bits of marzipan, and model it into the shapes of your favorite flowers.

**2** You can use toothpicks to help keep the flowers and leaves together.

**3** Paint the daisy petals and leaves with food coloring, and allow them to dry. They are delicious and make great cake decorations, too.

**Hint:** Many large supermarkets sell marzipan, which is a mixture of ground almonds, egg white, and sugar—sometimes it's in the candy section. If you can't find it, try looking for a can of almond paste that has the recipe on the side.

# Artful Sandwiches

**Type of Activity:** Painting
**Object:** Make sandwiches that feast the eyes too
**Ages:** 8 and older

**Materials Needed:**
• Milk
• Four paper cups
• Red, blue, green, and yellow food coloring
• Small, perfectly clean paintbrushes
• White bread
• A toaster
• Your favorite sandwich filling

**1** Put a few drops of milk and a few drops of a different food coloring into each of the four cups.

**2** Paint a picture or design with the milk-paints on two slices of bread for each sandwich. Don't get the bread soggy, though.

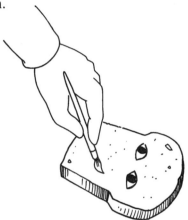

**3** Toast the bread lightly.

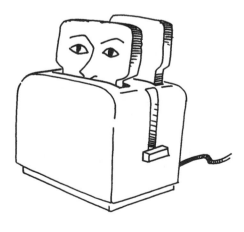

**4** Build your sandwich, eat, enjoy!

**Hint:** This makes a great activity and food for a party.

# Tempera Cookie Art

**Type of Activity:** Painting and baking
**Object:** Create a unique jumbo-cookie painting
**Ages:** 8 and older—*Adult Supervision*

**Materials Needed:**
• Well-chilled cookie dough (see Hint)
• Waxed paper
• A rolling pin
• A dinner knife
• Three beaten egg yolks
• Four small paper cups
• Red, yellow, blue, and green food coloring
• Spoons
• A nonstick cookie sheet
• A toothpick
• A perfectly clean paintbrush

**1** Pinch off a lump of dough about the size of a tennis ball. On the waxed paper, use the rolling pin to roll the lump until it's about ¼-inch thick and roughly rectangular or square.

**2** With the knife, trim the sides of the dough. Then put the dough in the fridge.

**3** Divide the egg yolk evenly among the four cups, and add several drops of a different food coloring to each. Stir.

**4** Remove the dough from the fridge and put it on your cookie sheet. Preheat the oven to 375°F. Use a toothpick to sketch a picture or design on the dough. Then paint in the colors with the dyed yolks.

**5** Bake 13 to 15 minutes at 375°F. Cool, display, and (eventually) eat!

**Hint:** Most supermarkets sell plain sugar-cookie dough in tubes in the refrigerated-foods section or you can mix your own using the recipe on page 220. Don't add chocolate chips or candies or anything like that.

# Cathedral Cookies

**Type of Activity:** Baking
**Object:** Create cookies with stained glass windows
**Ages:** 9 and older—*Adult Supervision*

**Materials Needed:**
• Cookie dough (see Hint)
• Waxed paper
• Heavy duty tinfoil
• Vegetable oil
• A cookie sheet
• Clear hard candies (ones you can see light through) broken in bits

**1** Preheat the oven to 375°F. Break off lumps of dough (tennis-ball size) and, on the waxed paper, roll them into ropes.

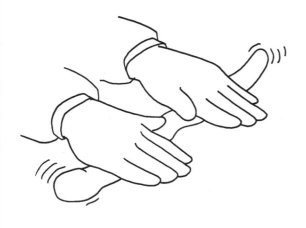

**2** Use these ropes to form the outline of your mini-cathedrals. Don't make the openings for the "glass" too large.

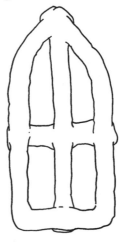

**3** Place the shaped dough on tinfoil (oiled lightly) on the cookie sheet, and bake for 5 minutes at 375°F. Remove them from the oven, but leave the oven on, and leave the cookies on the foil.

**4** When the shapes are cool, fill the openings with the broken candies.

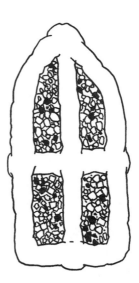

**5** Return the cookies to the oven. Check after 3 minutes, then check every minute. When the dough is light brown and all the candy is melted, take them out of the oven. (Be careful not to overcook because the candy could melt away or burn.)

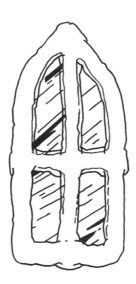

**Hint:** Some premade sugar cookie dough from the supermarket will work fine for this project. You can also make your own dough. The dough made from the recipe in the following activity will form easily into "ropes." This recipe may make more dough than you want; however, you may make mistakes or may have to experiment with cooking times to suit your oven or the candy you've chosen. To avoid waste, make one cookie at a time, and keep the dough in the fridge in the meantime.

# Do Your Own Dough

**Type of Activity:** Recipe following and baking

**Object:** Create dough for Cathedral Cookies and Tempera Cookies

**Ages:** 8 and older—*Adult Supervision*

**Materials Needed:**
- Measuring cups and spoons
- 1 cup (2 sticks) of butter, softened
- 1 cup of sugar
- A large mixing bowl
- A stirring spoon *or* rubber spatula
- Two eggs
- 3½ cups of all-purpose flour
- 1 teaspoon of baking powder
- 1 teaspoon of salt
- 2 teaspoons of vanilla extract
- Waxed paper
- A cookie sheet, greased, or nonstick
- A fork
- Candy sprinkles (optional)

**1** Blend the butter and sugar in the bowl, then blend in the eggs, flour, baking powder, salt, and vanilla. Cover with waxed paper and refrigerate the dough for several hours.

**2** To make simple cookies with this dough, pinch off small lumps and roll them into balls with your hands.

**3** Place the balls in rows on the cookie sheet. Press each one flat with a fork. Decorate the cookies with candy sprinkles if you like.

**4** Bake about 10 minutes at 375°F or until the cookies are golden brown.

# Monster Mosaic Salad

**Type of Activity:** Assembly cooking
**Object:** Make a beautiful side salad
**Ages:** 8 and older—*Adult Supervision*

**Materials Needed:**
- A measuring cup
- Mosaic bits: approximately 1 cup each of fruits, nuts, and vegetables (see step 1)
- A knife and cutting board
- Water
- A saucepan
- A shallow round cake pan (metal only) and a slightly larger plate (see step 8)
- A mixing bowl
- Two 3-ounce packages of lemon, lime, *or* orange gelatin dessert
- A spoon
- 1 cup of cottage cheese
- ½ cup of mayonnaise

**1** Mosaic bits can include: slivered almonds, broken walnuts, carrots, celery, black olives, bell pepper (red, green, or orange), purple cabbage, maraschino cherries—check out your fridge and cabinets. Chop up heaps of each, all in bits about the same size.

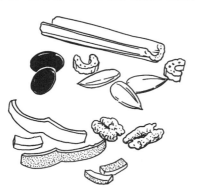

**2** Put 1½ cups of water on to boil. Meanwhile, using your palette of vegetable bits, create in the bottom of the cake pan your monster's face or other design— flowers are another nice choice.

**3** Empty both packs of gelatin into the boiling water. Stir until the granules are dissolved, remove from heat, then add a cup of very cold water. The mixture will thicken just slightly.

**4** Slowly, carefully spoon gelatin onto the monster's face. Put just enough in the bottom so the bits will adhere as the gelatin solidifies. Don't put in enough to float the bits.

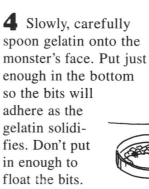

**5** Carefully place the pan in the fridge. Use a table knife to replace any pieces that dislodge. Put the pan of leftover gelatin mixture in the fridge, too.

**6** After an hour, bring out the leftover gel mixture and mix it with the cottage cheese and mayo. Pour this over the monster, and refrigerate the pan overnight (or at least several hours).

**7** After it's well-chilled, remove the pan from the fridge and place it in hot water for 10 seconds. (Make sure not to let water into the pan.)

**8** Cover the pan with a plate and turn it upside down. Shake it gently, set down, and pull the pan up.

**9** There he is!

# Pretzel Serpent

**Type of Activity:** Sculpting and baking
**Object:** Make a handsome snake that you can bite
**Ages:** 9 and older—*Adult Supervision*

**Materials Needed:**
• Measuring cups and spoons
• 1 cup of warm water
• A package of dry yeast
• 1 teaspoon of sugar
• 1 teaspoon of salt
• 3½ cups of all-purpose flour
• A large mixing bowl
• A stirring spoon *or* rubber spatula
• One egg
• Coarse salt
• Vegetable oil
• A clean dish cloth
• Poppy seeds, caraway seeds, candy bits, *or* a combination of several of these
• A cookie sheet, greased or nonstick

**1** In the large mixing bowl, combine the water, yeast, sugar, salt, egg, oil, and 1 cup of flour. Blend until smooth.

**2** Put the rest of the flour in a mound on the table or counter. Make an opening in the middle, so it looks like a volcano. Pour the liquid from step 1 into the volcano's mouth.

**3** Use your fingers to mix the flour into the liquid bit by bit until dough forms.

**4** Fold the dough in on itself. Make a quarter turn, and fold again. (This is kneading.) Knead the dough for 10 minutes. Flour your fingers and the table lightly if they get sticky. Keep kneading until the dough is smooth and elastic.

**5** Put the dough in a bowl, cover it with a damp cloth, and set it in a warm corner of the kitchen for at least 1 hour and not more than 2. It should rise up and be high and puffy.

**6** After the dough has risen, preheat the oven to 475°F. Punch the dough with your fist until all the air goes out of it. It is now ready to be sculpted.

**7** Roll out the serpent, and decorate it with seeds or candies.

**8** Place it on the cookie sheet, and bake for about 15 minutes. Get out the butter, cheese, mustard, or whatever you like with pretzels, and enjoy.

# Deco Ice Pops

**Materials Needed:**
- An ice tray
- Your favorite juice *or* other beverage, such as Kool-Aid
- Blueberries and strawberries, and ripe melon cut into berry-size bits; *or* your own favorite fruit

**Type of Activity:** Mixing
**Object:** Make pretty icy summer snacks
**Ages:** 7 and older

**1** Put a generous dollop of fruit bits in each section of the ice tray.

**2** Fill the tray with fruit juice.

**3** Put the tray in the freezer overnight.

**4** Pop them out, and eat as desired or use them as ice cubes in a glass of water or lemonade.

# Great Graham Party Treats

**Type of Activity:** Assembling
**Object:** Make fun and sweet party treats
**Ages:** 7 and older

**Materials Needed:**
- A measuring cup and a teaspoon
- Milk
- Powdered sugar
- A small bowl
- Plain *or* chocolate graham crackers
- A variety of small candies (chocolate chips, jelly beans, M&Ms, and so on)
- Glittery candy sprinkles

**1** Mix "glue" by combining a teaspoon of milk in ¼ cup of powdered sugar.

**2** Arrange candies into fun pictures on the crackers. Glue them down.

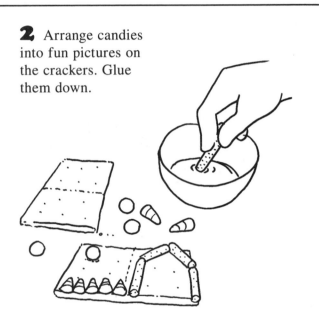

**3** You could also make a candy design, such as a flower, on one side of the cracker. Then, use "glue" covered with sprinkles to write initials on the other half to create unique place cards!

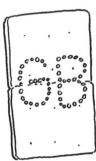

## Variation:

Use stoned-wheat crackers and unsweetened cereal bits, mini-pretzels, popcorn, nuts, and seeds for a salty version.

# V. Fabric, Yarn, Ribbon, and String

# Instant String Basket

**Materials Needed:**
- A paper bowl, the largest you can find
- White glue in a squeeze bottle *or* a container of glue and a brush
- A spool of hemp *or* other "hairy" or otherwise attractive twine or light rope

**Type of Activity:**  Assembling and gluing
**Object:**  Make an attractive hemp basket
**Ages:**  8 and older

**1** Swirl or brush glue in the bottom of the bowl.  Starting in the center of the bottom, begin lining the bowl with concentric circles of string.

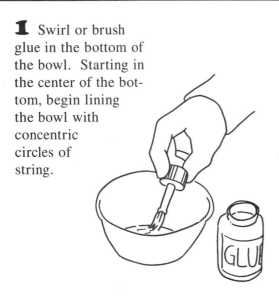

**2** Continue up the sides of the bowl, applying glue and laying the string down. As you go, press the string gently in place, keeping successive circles parallel and straight.

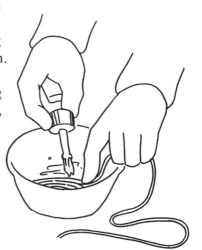

**3** When you reach the top of the rim, let the glue dry for a few minutes. Then flip the bowl over and continue on the outside.

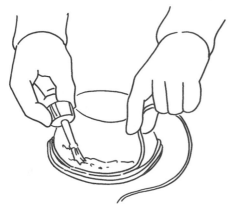

**4** When it has dried completely, you have a beautiful holder for fruit or shells.

# Yarn Art Picture

**Type of Activity:** Artful assembling
**Object:** Draw a picture with yarn
**Ages:** 8 and older

**Materials Needed:**
- A sheet of stiff cardboard *or* light, smooth wood paneling
- A pencil
- Many colors of yarn: wool, cotton, or synthetic
- Scissors
- White glue in a squeeze bottle *or* a container of glue and a brush

**1** Draw a design on the cardboard. A symmetrical design is good, and simple will look best.

**2** Cut a length of yarn for one part of the design. Lay it over the pencil drawing to see how it will look. Squeeze (or brush) some glue along that part of the design.

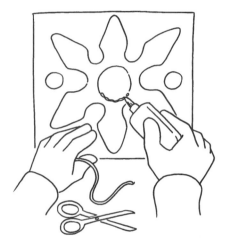

**3** Continue cutting lengths of yarn and gluing them to the design. In areas where you have lines of string together, use contrasting (light and dark) colors.

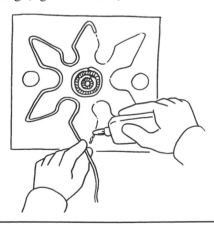

**4** Continue until you've finished your bright and unique picture.

# Cord-Twist Trivet

**Type of Activity:** String and fabric twining and twisting

**Object:** Make an attractive hot plate

**Ages:** 9 and older

**Materials Needed:**
- Cotton or cotton/polyester fabric, about a foot wide and a yard long (see step 1)
- A tape measure *or* ruler
- A 7-foot-or-so length of hemp twine, cotton cord, *or* thick lightweight rope
- Scissors

**1** You could also use several pieces of foot-wide fabric of different colors and textures, as long as you have a total of a yard or more of fabric. The fabric (or fabrics) you choose must be thin enough to be tearable. Test it by cutting a notch about ¾ of an inch from one edge. Tear straight down, resulting in a foot-long strip. Tear all the fabric into ¾ inch-wide strips.

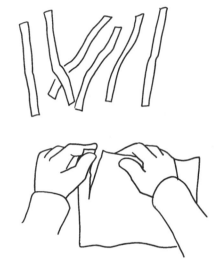

**2** Cut one end of your rope at an angle. To fasten the first strip of fabric to one end of the rope: Loop the fabric around the first 2 inches of the rope, and begin circling the rope and covering the tag end of the fabric at the same time.

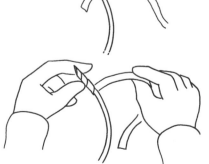

**3** Cover about 4 inches of the rope with fabric, then stop and begin turning the covered part of the rope into a circle. With what's left of your fabric strip, loop back through the beginning part of the rope, connecting it to the next uncovered bit of rope.

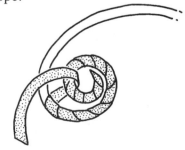

**4** Continue encircling the rope with fabric. Stop every couple of inches to bend the rope in a circle, running a loop of fabric back through the previous circle of rope (A); where you reach the end of the rope, cut it at an angle. Wrap this end tightly to the adjacent ring several times (B).

(A)  (B)

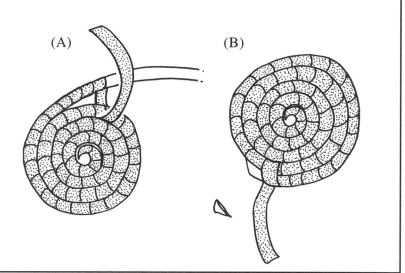

**5** You've got a great-looking hot plate.

# String-Collage Keepsake Box

**Type of Activity:** Assembling and gluing
**Object:** Make an attractive string-decorated keepsake box
**Ages:** 7 and older

**Materials Needed:**
• An empty cigar box *or* other sturdy, lidded cardboard box
• A paintbrush
• Paint
• Scrap paper
• A pencil
• About a yard each of at least three different types of hemp twine, cotton cord, light rope, string, *or* yarn
• Glue

**1** Paint your box the color of your choice. Set it aside to dry. Repeat with more coats until any writing or decorations are completely covered.

**2** On the paper, draw a shape about the size of the lid of your box. Then sketch in the picture that you want to create with string.

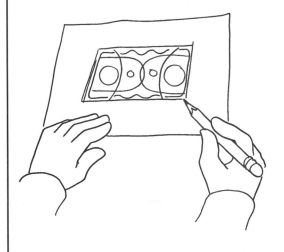

**3** When the box is completely dry, begin cutting pieces of string. Glue them down to the box lid, copying your drawing. You may incorporate a handle, but make sure to glue it very securely.

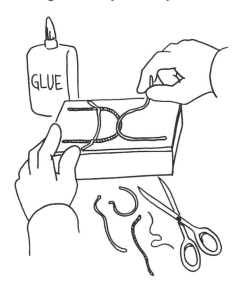

**4** When you are finished, you have a great storage box tailored for you . . .

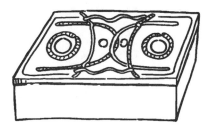

**5** . . . or for a Mother's Day gift.

# Finger-Weave Belt

**Materials Needed:**
- A 4-yard piece of cotton rope or round ribbon or cord, *or* strips of scrap leather, *or* suede
- Bells, shells, large beads (for Variation)

**Type of Activity:** Weaving
**Object:** Make a simple belt
**Ages:** 8 and older

**1** Near the end of the rope, tie a loose knot. The opening in the knot should be big enough for you to insert your thumb.

**2** Loop the other end of the rope back through this opening, exactly as shown. This is the basic building block of finger weaving (A). Repeat, looping through the first circle, and the second (B).

(A)     (B)

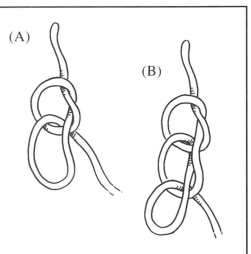

**3** Continue finger-braiding—trying to keep the size of the knot openings even—until you have a length braided that's long enough to circle your waist and to tie.

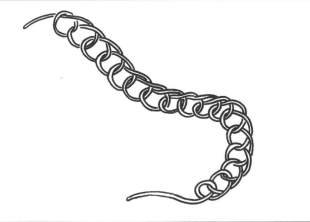

**4** Knot each end to keep it from unraveling. Cut off any excess.

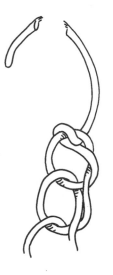

**Variation:**
Tie bells, shells, or large beads to the end of your belt instead of simply knotting the ends.

# Weaving

**Type of Activity:** Assembling and weaving
**Object:** Make a loom and weave a pot holder and a mitt
**Ages:** 10 and older

## #1 Pot Holder

**Materials Needed:**
- About 12 large (adult), heavy socks in many colors
- Scissors
- 3 or more large (adult), thinner socks in one color
- A sheet of heavy cardboard, 7 by 9 inches
- A pencil
- A ruler
- Large paper clips

**1** From the leg part (not the feet) of the heavier socks, cut 14 rings about ½ inch wide. Also cut one long, ¾ inch-wide strip from one thin sock by cutting down the leg and foot in a spiral.

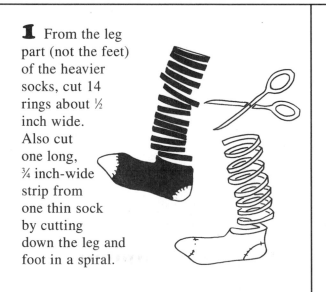

**2** On both 9-inch sides of the cardboard, starting an inch from each side, measure, mark, and cut ½-inch-long lines, ¼ inch apart. You'll end up with 29 notches on top and bottom. This is the loom.

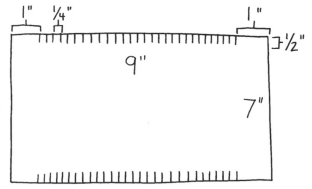

**3** Now stretch one ring down the front of the loom by looping it onto the first "tab" at the top—the one formed by the first and second notches—and stretching it down to that same tab on bottom. Stretch another ring down the front of the loom from the second tab on top to the second tab on bottom. Continue until all 14 rings are stretched on the front of the loom. You now have the warp portion of your weaving.

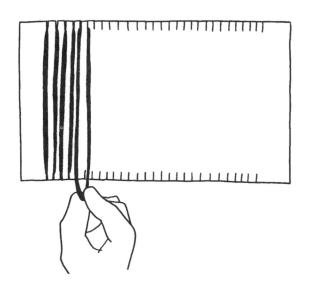

**4** Thread one end of your thin-sock strip onto a paper clip. This is the weaver. Tie the other end of the strip to the top of one of the side warp rings on the loom.

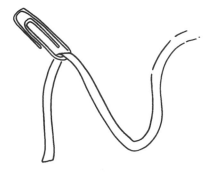

**5** Begin weaving. Start as close to the top of the tabs as you can without dislodging the warp. As shown, go over one warp ring, under the next, over the next. At the end of the row, turn and start back. If you run out of weaver strip, knot another one onto the end of the one you just finished, and keep weaving.

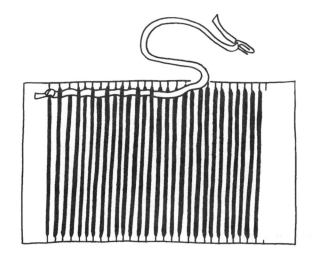

**6** At the end of the last row, slip the pot holder off of the loom. Slide all the weave strips down snugly against the loop ends where you began. With the holder off the loom, continue weaving the unfinished edge, snugly, all the way to edge.

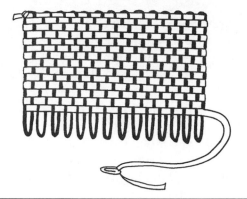

**7** At the end, tie the weaver securely to one of the side rings, and snip off the excess. Your pot holder is ready to use!

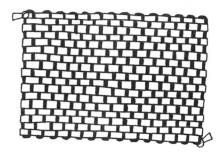

## #2  Mitt

**1** From the leg parts of the heavier socks, cut 29 rings about ½ inch wide. Cut two thin socks down the leg and foot, in a spiral, into two long strips about ¾ inch wide.

**2** Using the same loom you made for the pot holder, make your warp: Stretch one of the 29 rings around the loom, front and back. Secure it from the first notch on the top to the first notch on the bottom. Stretch another ring around the cardboard, secured in the second notches on top and bottom. Continue until all the rings are stretched, parallel to each other, around the cardboard. Alternate colors if you like.

**3** To make the weaver, thread one end of your thin-sock strip onto the paper clip. Tie the other end of the strip to the top of one of the side rings on the loom. This is the weaver.

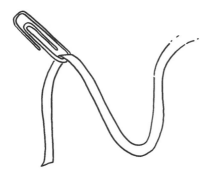

**4** Begin weaving. Go over one warp ring, under the next, over the next. At the end of the row, turn and start back. (If you run out of weaver strip, knot another one onto the end of the one you just finished, and keep weaving. Oops! If your thin socks were short, you may have to go find another to cut up.)

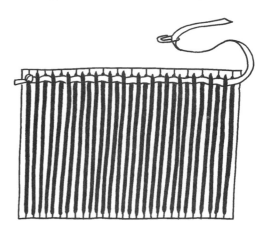

**5** Weave all the way to the bottom, keeping the weave tight. At the bottom of the loom, flip the loom over and weave the warp on the other side.

**6** When both sides are complete, and the weave is consistently tight, tie the weaver off at one of the side rings, and cut the excess.

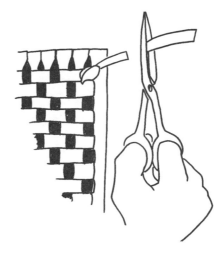

**7** Bend the cardboard, and slip the mitt off.

**8** Thread the paper clip with another long strip. Sew together one of the 7-inch sides in an "overcast stitch": Use the clip—exactly as you would a needle—to pierce a ring, loop over the side, pierce, loop, and so on, along one entire side. This closes the end, turning the tube you had into a pocket.

**9** Slip your hand in and use the mitt to handle hot stuff.

# Mat Weaving

**Type of Activity:** Cutting and weaving
**Object:** Create a colorful place mat
**Ages:** 9 and older

**Materials Needed:**
- Patterned (floral, paisley, or other) shelf liner paper *or* oil cloth (should be waterproof) and a solid-colored, 12-by-18-inch piece of thick shelf paper *or* oil cloth (waterproof)
- A ruler
- Scissors *or* a utility knife
- A pencil
- Glue
- Cloth *or* paper towels for wiping glue

---

**1** Cut the patterned shelf paper into ten 1-by-16-inch strips.

**2** On the large rectangle of solid-colored shelf paper, draw 17 lines, 1 inch apart and 1 inch from each edge. Cut these lines open, leaving a 1-inch border intact.

**3** Starting 1 inch into the rectangle (inside the border), weave one of the 1-by-16-inch patterned strips through the slits of the mat, alternating the patterned strip over and under the solid bar.

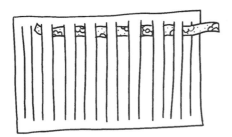

**4** When finished, push the strip against the border and straighten it. Glue both ends of the strip down securely; press firmly for a few seconds, then wipe off any excess glue.

**5** Weave the second strip so that the in-and-out of the pattern alternates with that of the first strip. Continue weaving and gluing all the strips, alternating them. Always make sure to glue the edges of the strips down well and wipe off any excess glue.

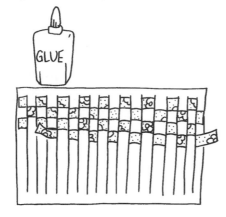

**6** An attractive and practical place mat! (To clean, wipe with a damp cloth.)

# Quick Basket

**Type of Activity:** Milk jug basket
**Object:** Create a cloth and plastic basket
**Ages:** 8 and older—*Adult Supervision*

**Materials Needed:**
- A 1-gallon plastic milk jug, washed and with the label removed
- A grease pencil, crayon, *or* soft pencil
- A ruler
- Scissors
- Several pieces of solid-colored cloth and several pieces with different patterns (see step 2)
- One piece of cloth at least 23 inches long
- Glue

**1** Draw lines on the jug bottom as shown, starting ½ inch from the bottom; make them ¾ inch apart. Cut through each line. Most milk jugs have a circumference of 22 inches; if yours does, you will cut 28 bands, the last one slightly wider than the others.

**2** Choose pieces of cloth at least 7 inches wide; length doesn't matter. The fabric (cotton or cotton blend ) should be thick enough that you can put a little of your glue on one side without its bleeding through. Cut all your cloth into ¾-inch strips at least 7 inches long.

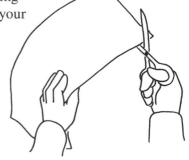

**3** Measure one of the vertical bands on the jug from the bottom of the cut, up the front, over the top, and down to the start of the cut on the inside. It should measure about 6 inches. Trim 28 solid-colored cloth strips to this length. One by one, glue the cloth strips up the front of the bands, over the top, and down the inside. Spread the glue lightly so it doesn't bleed through the fabric.

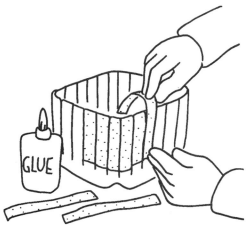

**4** Begin weaving strips of patterned fabrics horizontally through the vertical bands.

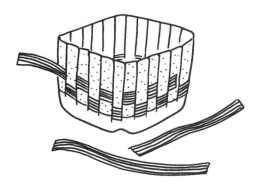

**5** When you reach the top edge, cut a 23-inch strip (2 inches wide or so) from your long piece of fabric. Fold this over the edge and lightly glue it down, over-lapping its two ends.

**6** Your basket is gorgeous—and waterproof on the bottom. You can use it for a planter or a holder for just about anything.

241

# Braid a Coaster

**Materials Needed:**
- Cotton yarn *or* light rope, three 4-foot-long strands for each coaster, all the same or different colors
- A clipboard
- An embroidery needle threaded with a long piece of embroidery thread in a complementary color to the yarn

**Type of Activity:** Three-strand braiding
**Object:** Make a protective coaster
**Ages:** 9 and older

---

**1** Put one end of each of the three strands of yarn under the clip of the clipboard.

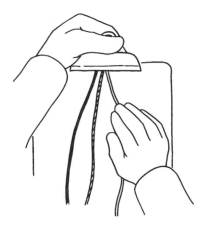

**2** Begin braiding the three strands together. Three-strand braiding is simple. Cross the outside strand on the right over the middle strand; then cross the outside strand on the left over the middle; then the right again and left again to the end of the strands.

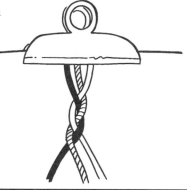

**3** When you've braided down to the bottom, remove the yarn from the clip. With the needle and thread, stitch both ends into points so they won't unbraid.

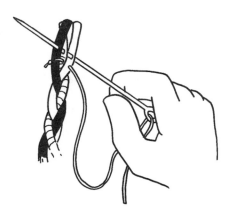

**4** Begin turning your braid around on itself in a circle. Keeping the braid flat, stitch the starting point of the braid to the circle of braid that now encloses it.

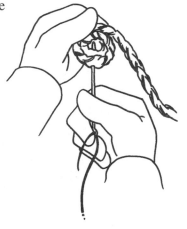

**5** Continue curling the braid in a circle. Every inch or so, stitch the outer circle to the inner one.

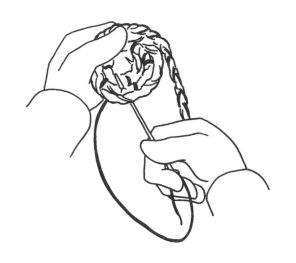

**6** Your coaster is flat and attractive, and it will protect the table. You can make a set for a gift.

# Braid a Leash

**Type of Activity:** Four-strand braiding
**Object:** Make a very strong leash for your pet
**Ages:** 9 and older

**Materials Needed:**
- Two 15-foot strands of macramé cord in contrasting colors and a 1-yard strand in a third color
- A clip for attaching the cord to a dog collar (from a craft store)
- A clipboard

**1** Put the two long strands of cord side by side. Bend them over in the center of their length and pull them through the clip. Put the clip in the clipboard. Arrange the strands so that the colors are light, light, dark, dark.

**2** Start braiding just beneath the clip. Pick up the outside dark strand on the right. Pull it under the inside dark and the inside light strands, then carry it back over the inside light strand and to the right. Place it between the light and dark strands (A). Now take the outside light strand from the left, carry it under the inside light and dark strands, then back over the inside dark strand and to the left. Place it between the light and dark strands (B).

(A)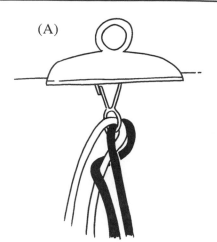

(B)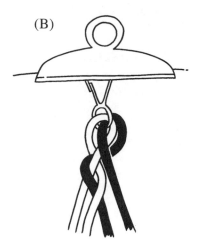

**3** Continue in the same manner, weaving the four strands to their ends.

**4** Fold the end of the braid in a loop that fits your hand.

**5** Pull your 1-yard strand of cord halfway through the loop and wrap it tightly, moving away from the handle loop, binding together about 4 inches of overlapping leash.

**6** Ready to take Bowser for a walk.

# Five T-Shirt Decorating Projects

**Type of Activity:** Gluing, sewing, dyeing, and more

**Object:** Make ordinary T-shirts extraordinary

**Ages:** 10 and older

**Materials Needed:**
- A sheet of plastic to cover your work area
- A T-shirt—white or colored (plan for good contrast between the paint you choose for a project and the shirt's color): it should be plain (without decorations) and 100% cotton; it can be new or old, but it must have been washed and dried at least once
- Additional materials for each project

## #1 Tie Dye It

**Additional Materials Needed:**
- Fiber-reactive dye (one or more colors) and dye fixer (both available in fabric and sewing stores)
- Large and small disposable containers for mixing dyes
- Stirring spoons
- Rubber gloves
- Rubber bands, small and large
- A plastic bag
- Water
- Dishwashing liquid
- A clothesline and clothespins
- A long piece of thick, sturdy string (for Variation)

**1** Spread plastic over your work surface. Mix the dye according to directions. In the larger container, mix the fixer according to directions. Put the T-shirt in the fixer and leave it for 30 minutes.

**2** Put on your gloves and wring out the shirt. Then spread it smooth out on the plastic-covered surface.

**3** Fold the shirt back and forth on itself in an accordion fashion (A), then bind it tightly with evenly spaced rubber bands (B).

(A)

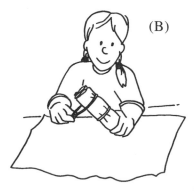
(B)

**4** With the bundle on its side, pour a little dye (one color or alternating different colors) onto the shirt right at the rubber bands.

**5** Put the shirt in a plastic bag and leave it for 3 days. At the end of this time, rinse the bundled shirt repeatedly until the water runs clear. Then take the bands off and rinse more, again until the water runs clear.

**6** Soak the shirt for 10 minutes in a sink of hot, soapy water. Rinse it with cold water until the water runs clear.

**7** Line dry your shirt, and it's ready to wear.

## Variation:

**1** Knot string onto one corner of the shirt.

**2** Crumple part of the shirt, and bind it tightly with string. Crumple it again, and bind it with string. Keep going until the whole shirt is tightly crumpled and tied.

**3** Dip the shirt into a container of dye for no more than a minute (less time makes lighter colors). Repeat steps 5 to 7 for a shirt of veins and star bursts.

# #2 Paint and Dye It

**Additional Materials Needed:**
- Fiber-reactive dye and dye fixer (both available in fabric and sewing stores)
- A large and a small disposable container for fixer and the dye
- Stirring spoons
- Rubber gloves
- Newspaper
- Fabric paint in a squeeze bottle
- A small spoon

**1** Spread plastic over your work surface. In the small container, mix the fiber-reactive dye, and in the large container, mix the fixer, both according to directions. Put your shirt in the fixer and leave it for 30 minutes. Then put on the rubber gloves and wring it out. Place it on the plastic to dry.

**2** When the shirt's dry, spread it flat and stuff it with many layers (2 inches deep at least) of clean, dry, flat newspaper.

**3** Wearing your rubber gloves, use the fabric paint to draw the outline of your design.

**4** With the small spoon, add the liquid dye to fill in the shapes of your design. Bleeding over the outline of the paint with dye is part of this technique's special look.

**5** Keep painting and dyeing until you have a T-shirt of a unique design.

# #3 Wild Paint Job

**Additional Materials Needed:**
- Newspaper
- Several colors of fabric paint in a squeeze bottle and several colors of fabric paint in open-mouth containers
- A stick
- A dry sponge
- A plastic pot scrubby
- A flat paintbrush

**1** Smooth your shirt out on a plastic-covered work surface, and stuff it with many layers (2 inches deep at least) of clean, dry, flat newspaper.

**2** Now the fun begins. The object is to cover your shirt with a wild design of paint. You can drip paint onto the surface straight from the squeeze bottle.

**3** Or, you can dip your stick in the paint and drizzle out a pattern. Use one color and then another.

**4** Or, you can dip your fingertips into paint and use them to flick paint onto the shirt. Use many colors or just one.

**5** Or, you can use the side of a flat brush, a dry sponge, or a pot scrubber (or other such "printer") to print texture on the shirt.

**6** You've got a one-of-a-kind shirt! (When it's thoroughly dry, turn it over and do the back if you like.)

**Hint:** It's a good idea to practice techniques on newspaper before starting on the final shirt product.

## Variation:

With a plain pair of cotton sneakers, you can make drizzle, splatter, or sponge shoes, too!

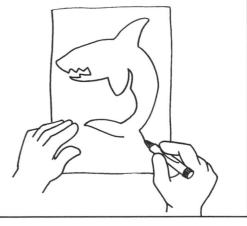

# #4 Stencil It

**Additional Materials Needed:**
- Stiff freezer paper
- Scissors
- A grease pencil *or* crayon
- Newspaper
- A bit of sponge
- Latex, acrylic, *or* fabric paint, in a color that contrasts with your T-shirt (light on dark, or vice versa)

**1** For your stencil, cut a square out of freezer paper that fits nicely on the front of your T-shirt. On the paper, draw a design.

**2** Cut the design out from the freezer paper. The square with the cutout is your stencil.

**3** Spread plastic over your work area. Put folded newspapers inside the shirt, and then spread the freezer paper out on the shirt.

**4** Use the sponge to dab paint into the openings of the stencil.

**5** Pull the stencil up and you've got a great-looking design on your shirt. Set aside or hang until dry.

## Variation:

**1** Cut a square of freezer paper as in the preceding step 1 and fold it in half and then in half again. Trim the edge into a curve.

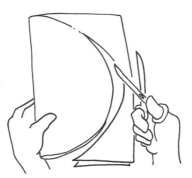

**2** Cut bits and pieces out of the sides and center of the folded up circle.

**3** Repeat steps 3 and 4 from the preceding instructions, using this stencil. Lift up the stencil and see your beautiful new shirt.

## #5 Stitch It

**Additional Materials Needed:**
- Buttons, bits of fabric, ribbon, sequins, lace, zipper parts, and any other odds and ends from the sewing drawer
- A pencil *or* washable marker
- Scissors
- A needle and thread
- Fabric glue
- Fabric paint in a squeeze bottle

**1** To make a picture or decoration on your shirt with your buttons, sequins, and so on, first draw the design on the shirt.

**2** Next, arrange your sewing bits on your drawing.

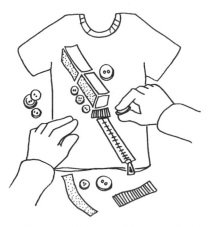

**3** Finally, attach your bits. You can sew some on and glue on some others.

**4** You can also add finishing touches to your design with fabric paint.

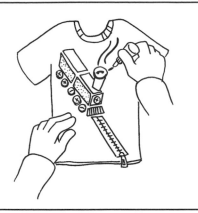

**Variation:**
With a plain pair of cotton sneakers, you can stitch or glue the same kinds of odds and ends to make wacky shoes, too!

# Beautiful Batik

**Type of Activity:** Fabric dyeing
**Object:** Make a beautiful and complex pattern with dye
**Ages:** 9 and older—*Adult Supervision*

**Materials Needed:**
• A square of clean, solid wax
• A clean empty coffee can that fits in your saucepan
• A saucepan of water
• A sheet of plastic to cover your work area
• Cotton fabric, white or light colored, about 1½ feet square, that has been washed and dried
• A pencil
• An old paintbrush
• Two colors of liquid dye
• A measuring cup and a tablespoon
• A bucket
• A stirring spoon
• Water
• Salt
• A clothesline and clothespins
• Blank newsprint-type paper
• An iron

**1** Put the wax in the coffee can, then put the can in the saucepan. Heat the saucepan on the stove until the wax melts.

**2** Spread plastic over your work area. Spread the fabric out, and draw a pattern or picture on the cloth. Decide which parts you want to be the lighter color dye, which parts the darker, and which parts will be undyed (keeping the original cloth color).

**3** Brush the liquid wax on the part that you want to remain undyed. The wax should soak through the cloth thoroughly. Allow the wax to harden.

**4** Mix ¼ cup of the lighter of the two dyes in the bucket with a gallon of hot water and a tablespoon of salt. Put the cloth in the bucket and let it soak for at least 30 minutes.

**5** Rinse the cloth in warmish water until the water runs clear, then hang it up to dry.

**6** When the cloth is dry, paint it with more wax (reheating the wax if necessary). This time, put wax on the areas where you want to preserve the light dye color, then let the wax harden. (The wax remains on the undyed parts as well.)

**7** Rinse the bucket out thoroughly and mix the second dye as you did in step 4. Put the cloth in the bucket again for 30 minutes, then rinse as you did in step 5.

**8** Place the cloth between layers of blank newsprint. Iron it repeatedly, changing the paper, until the ironing no longer causes wax stains on the paper. (This gets the wax out of the cloth.)

**9** Wash the cloth in hot soapy water, and hang it to dry.

**Hint:** The longer the cloth stays in the dye, the more intense the color. Also consider, when you choose the colors of dye, that the second color (step 7) will be dying parts of the cloth that were already dyed with a lighter color in step 4. The final color that results from the second dying will be affected by the underlying color—blue over yellow may be green-tinged; red over blue will be purplish.

# Towel Toga

**Type of Activity:** Simple sewing
**Object:** Make a quick and nifty cover-up for beach or bath
**Ages:** 9 and older—*Adult Supervision*

**Materials Needed:**
• A large old or new beach towel or bath towel
• Scissors
• A long strand of iron-on hem tape
• Straight pins
• An iron
• Thin yarn *or* heavy-duty embroidery thread
• A large needle that will work with your yarn or thread

**1** Fold the towel in half width-wise. Cut a slit in the fold, just large enough to slip your head through.

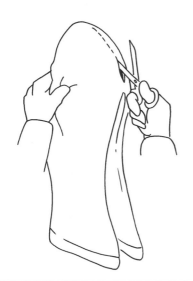

**2** Fold strips of the hem tape over the edges of the slit. Pin it into place at each end.

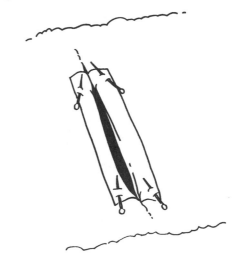

**3** Iron the hem tape according to package directions, removing the pins as you go until the neck opening is all hemmed.

**4** If the towel has a prettier side, turn it inside out. Begin stitching one side together from the bottom up. Thread the needle with the thread or yarn and knot it. Pierce through both layers just at the edge, looping over the two edges and piercing again in an "overcast stitch." Make a stitch only every inch or so. Go up the side far enough to leave a comfortable arm hole.

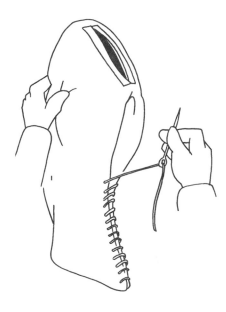

**5** Complete the stitching on both sides, then turn the cover-up right side out and pull it over your head.

**Hint:** Choose thread or yard that complements the towel.